11-18-68

# preface to parish renewal

# Wallace E. Fisher

# preface
# to
# parish
# renewal

ABINGDON PRESS  NASHVILLE AND NEW YORK

PREFACE TO PARISH RENEWAL

*Copyright © 1968 by Abingdon Press*

All rights in this book are reserved.
No part of the book may be reproduced in any
manner whatsoever without written permission of
the publishers except brief quotations embodied in
critical articles or reviews. For information address
Abingdon Press, Nashville, Tennessee.

*Standard Book Number: 687-33909-X*
*Library of Congress Catalog Card Number: 68-25358*

Scripture quotations unless otherwise noted are from the
Revised Standard Version of the Bible, copyrighted 1946
and 1952 by the Division of Christian Education, National Council of Churches, and are used by permission.

Excerpts from *God and Word* by Gerhard Ebeling are used
here by permission of Fortress Press, Philadelphia, Pa.

The quotation of Jacques Barzun is from an address at a
symposium on "The University in America," and is used
here by permission of the Center for the Study of
Democratic Institutions, Santa Barbara, Calif.

The quotation of Daniel Callahan is from his article "The
Renewal Mess" in the March 3, 1967, issue of *Common-
weal*, and is used here by permission of the author and of
*Commonweal.*

SET UP, PRINTED, AND BOUND BY THE
PARTHENON PRESS, AT NASHVILLE,
TENNESSEE, UNITED STATES OF AMERICA

To my parents, Daniel and Rose Fisher, and my parents-in-law, Earl and Louise Stauffer, onetime lay officers in Christ's church, and the hundreds of thousands like them who, though often weary in the Lord's work, have never wearied of it

AND

To the thousands of parish pastors who, faithful in a few things in spite of buffetings and defeats, covet Jesus' generous judgment, "Well done, good and faithful servant."

# acknowledgments

In a concise summary of this sort it is impossible to list all the sources that I have used, or to acknowledge fully my debt to Christian and secular writers who have lighted my path, or to express adequately my gratitude to lay and clerical colleagues who have helped me over hard places. But the dedication, occasional footnotes, and following paragraph make a stab at it.

My secretary, Mrs. Arline S. Fellenbaum, deserves thanks for preparing the manuscript. Jack R. Hoffman, Larry L. Lehman, and William B. Helsel, associates at Trinity Church; Howard Keeley, Harald Sigmar, and John Schmidt, ministerial colleagues in Boston, Vancouver, Washington, and Buffalo; and these members in Trinity: Wilfred P. Bennett, Robert P. Desch, J. Frank Everett, Ruth Grigg Horting, Ann Haagen Musselman, Gilbert W. Vatter, Ann Bolbach White, and Robert H. Witmer, M.D., have read the manuscript offering valuable comments. My wife, Margaret, perceptive critic and steadfast supporter, knows better than anyone my debt to her. Our son, Mark, like most teen-agers in Trinity, heartens us by his loyalty to Christ's church.

WALLACE E. FISHER

# contents

# Contents

# Introduction

*I find all books too long.*
—VOLTAIRE

---

It is now evident that thousands of laymen and parish pastors in urban, suburban, and rural churches are struggling valiantly to break rigid traditions and fashion flexible institutional forms so that the parish can exercise Christ's ministry in the world and for the world. But the avalanche of books, press accounts, magazine articles, TV interviews, and denominational literature on "renewal" has confused some laymen.

The questions fairly bristle. Do serious theologians think that God is dead? Are the basic doctrines of the church false? Is the Bible beyond the layman's understanding? Can anyone demonstrate that the Faith has its roots in history? Is preaching outmoded? Does Christ bid church members follow him into racial ghettos, economic marketplaces, and the arenas where political decisions are made? Is Christianity a private affair? The conflicting answers to these and other questions strike many laymen as "confusion roughly organized."

Daniel Callahan has described renewal as a "mess" in his Roman Catholic Church. His appraisal is descriptive of Protestantism, too.

When there is more zeal for "open inquiry" into the meaning of Christ than there is for Christ; when there is more enthusiasm for "frank discussion" between priests and laymen than there is for the role of priest and layman; when there is more interest in the "integrity" half of the phrase "Christian integrity" than for the "Christian" half; when there is more commitment to the "honesty" part of the equation "honesty in the church" than the "Church" part—then a very significant shift has taken place. I am not for a moment saying this kind of shift is bad (or good); that is another question. I am only saying it is important we take notice of it and try to understand its meaning. My own theory is that it signifies a considerable loss of traditional Christian faith and hope. But I would also want to say, just as strongly, that it represents for many the only way they feel is left for them to hope that their Christianity will come back to life.[1]

It will be tragic if the splendid promise of new life in the church goes unrealized because we talk it to death or run it into the ground for lack of a sound strategy.

Denominational bodies—sobered by the ineffectiveness of their constituent congregations, stung by a barrage of criticism from within and without, and prodded by the mighty stirrings in the Roman Catholic Church—are overhauling their machinery, listening to secular man, dialoguing with one another, updating their confessions, and issuing calls to renewal. Equally exciting are the evidences of cooperative, multiple, and specialized ministries. These stirrings and experiments are heartening, but they do not get at the core of the problem. "The sin of the church is not that it has not reformed society, but that it has not realized self-renewal. Its sin is that it has not repented. Without repentance there cannot be renewal."[2]

[1] "The Renewal Mess," Commonweal, March 3, 1967, p. 622.
[2] Will D. Campbell, Race and the Renewal of the Church (Philadelphia: The Westminster Press, 1962), p. 4.

Renewal requires more than social realism, cooperative ministries, and hard-nosed leadership. Renewal requires the converted heart, the enlightened mind, the obedient will. Repentance and gospel faith, an expectant waiting on the Holy Spirit, and the humbling of self, parish, and denomination before God are the requisites for renewal. Too often, however, these elemental needs are played down, glossed over, or ignored in the renewal literature. Well-intentioned, serious, and empirical, the literature is methodological rather than substantive. It centers on tactics rather than strategy.

The Protestant churches are questioning their traditions, examining their structures, and challenging their members to get "where the action is." These are necessary tactics for parish renewal, but they *are* tactics. A strategy for renewal calls for new persons. This requires earnest wrestling with the Scriptures' witness to the Word, personal commitment, and costly discipleship. Renewal in the biblical sense calls for radical change in persons, which in turn calls for a redeployment of personnel in the local parish and in the ecclesiastical centers. Presently, Rome is deciding whether it wants to take renewal *that* seriously. Protestantism has not yet decided to decide. The denominations prefer to refine their ecclesiastical machinery, polish their tarnished images, and exhort their parishes to update their ministries. That is not enough. Radical change in persons and a fresh deployment of personnel is as essential to new life in the Protestant churches as it is in the Catholic Church.

This radical change in persons brings acute pain and deep travail for them and consequently for their parish and community. It breeds conflict among parishes in the same community where covert competition, suspicious coexistence, and fitful cooperation are daily realities. Renewal unites. It also divides. Protestantism finds this biblical truth too disruptive to face squarely. That is one reason why renewal is not sweeping the church. There are exciting exceptions here and there, but triviality and irrelevancy are still the marks of the grass-roots church.

My first two books—laboratory reports on twelve years of parish renewal in one setting—were written to encourage parish pastors and lay leaders.[3] This one is a study book for official board members, church school teachers, lay evangelists, members of women's societies, youth workers, prospective members, seminarians, parish pastors, and bishops who shepherd. It reflects two decades of ministry in suburban, college, and urban parishes. It incorporates the distilled insights and practical suggestions of several thousand Protestant churchmen (ordained and lay) in sixty or so conferences on parish renewal. It also profits from the judgments of Roman Catholic renewalists.

To read and talk about the mission of the church, dialogue with the world, the roles of clergy and laity, and the need for specialized and cooperative ministries (denominational and interdenominational) without facing concrete issues in one's own parish *and* community *and* denomination aborts church renewal. A

[3] *From Tradition to Mission* (Nashville: Abingdon Press, 1965); and *Preaching and Parish Renewal* (Abingdon Press, 1966).

competent layman on the official board of a congregation in the throes of renewal exploded: "This is one layman who is weary of 'leaders' in the church who analyze endlessly—and superficially—and come to *no* conclusions that result in meaningful action. I read and even become excited about Vatican II documents, for example, because, although the Catholics are saddled with some 'leaders' who use talk for delay and evasion, the documents nevertheless signal significant ferment and change. No intelligent person doubts the necessity and inevitability of analysis; the educated man cultivates an automatically critical frame of mind. But decisions must be made. Single steps toward an ultimate goal must be taken. Action is elemental to renewal."

On the other hand, as this layman knows, renewal does not come simply by decision and action. Affirmative response to the plea, "Let's get something done around here," will end in frustration unless (a) clean diagnoses lay bare the realities in the situation; (b) biblical goals and purposes are perceived, defined, and pursued; (c) the cost of discipleship is recognized and accepted; and (d) divine resources are claimed daily. Unless the renewal program reflects God's purposes for his people as discerned in the light of the Scriptures' witness and Christian history, and unless the parish leaders claim the gift of the Holy Spirit, the enactment of proposals and the implementation of programs will bring hurt without healing. Renewal requires passion *and* perspective. Jacques Barzun, challenging educators, speaks pungently to a deep-seated malaise in the institutional church:

Judging from what is being studied, researched, fact-found all over the world, it is clear that as a civilization we no longer know how to do anything. We can meet no situation, pursue no purpose, without stopping work and studying. Nor can we start up again without a period of exploration and testing. We are persuaded that nothing can be done today as it once was done. So we repeatedly analyze the familiar and suspend action. The upshot is that we are as helpless in the face of common needs as we are in the face of emergencies. We sit and wait for the reports to tell us what to do, and our self-consciousness grows faster than our knowledge or our will. Only our faith in progress, our faith in the automatism of our methods and our gadgets, keeps us in countenance. The paradox here is that turning the academic experts loose on the so-called problems of society tends toward the general paralysis. The mania for analyzing and investigating is one form of the well-recognized disorder known in psychiatry by the French name of *folie du doute.* The cure for the disease is obviously a philosophic review of means and ends. But the attempt would require detachment, a proper measure of idleness, and a liberal, as against a *professional,* outlook. And . . . these are the very attributes excluded by the modern design and impetus of the university.[4]

Passion without perspective can breed chaos. Perspective without passion can suspend action. Both are essential strands in parish renewal, as well as in university renewal. Creative leaders in all fields of human endeavor are loyal to some distant vision; they

[4] Speech at a symposium on "The University in America" sponsored by the Center for the Study of Democratic Institutions. Quoted in the *Council for Basic Education Bulletin,* March, 1967.

operate from a firm philosophical or religious base. Creative leadership requires a perspectival frame of reference for handling controversial but secondary issues. President Lincoln's decisions reflected his central intention to preserve the Union. The apostle Paul endured shipwreck, beatings, stonings, alienation, and rejection because he recognized that "weight of glory" with insight. Kurt Lewin, appointed to the Navy's Advisory Panel on Human Relations in 1945, insisted that there be "no research without action; no action without research." Jesus counseled those who were attracted to him to count the cost of discipleship; he also urged them to test his doctrine in daily living.

A generation of studies on the nature and mission of the church, secular man, and the art of communication—reflecting Protestant, Roman Catholic, sectarian, humanistic, and scientific insights—has produced a mass of uneven literature on the renewal of persons and institutions in general and on the church in particular.[5] Authenticated perspectives on church renewal can now be defined. A working guide for laymen is attempted in Chapter 1, "The Risk of Vulnerability." The title comes from an exciting conference with six hundred "conservative" clergy from eight denominations in New England.

Chapter 2, "By Whose Authority?" is as complex as it is crucial. But the question must be wrestled with in each parish if renewal is to happen there. Secular man acts egocentrically and justifies himself on prag-

---

[5] Renewal literature abounds in all fields. See, for example, John W. Gardner, *Self-Renewal* (New York: Harper & Row, 1961), and Marshall McLuhan, *Understanding Media: The Extensions of Man* (New York: Signet Books, 1964).

matic grounds. Christian man seeks to act for Christ and presents his apologetic in the light of his understanding of the Scriptures' witness to the Word of God. A primary question to be settled in every parish, therefore, concerns the nature and interpretation of the Scriptures' witness to the Word of God. Chapter 2 calls the renewalists to critical, existential Bible study and serious theological conversation. Biblical illiteracy, stultifying literalism, and do-it-yourself demythologization flourish in the American parish. The light of biblical scholarship must be focused there. The fundamentals of historical Christianity must be discerned objectively, taught relevantly, and acted on boldly by the laity. The Bible is the primary source for that. "The word of Holy Scripture discloses that which on a thousand occasions man may experience as his situation." The church must concentrate on the biblical Word of God "by stepping out into the world in confident reliance upon a new authority to speak." [6]

Chapter 3, "The Biblical Shape of the Church," is integrally related to Chapter 2. Christ is the Lord of the Scriptures. Equally, he is the Lord of the church. Chapter 2 points to the chart for parish renewal. Chapter 3 points to the compass. To set sail on the sea of renewal without both is to risk shipwreck or to cruise aimlessly.

The first three chapters, studied and discussed by lay leaders, will anger some and will sober many.

[6] Gerhard Ebeling, *God and Word*, trans. James W. Leitch (Philadelphia: Fortress Press, 1967), p. 48. This little book (53 pages) will help preachers, lay teachers, and lay evangelists to understand the Scriptures' witness to the Living Word.

Chapter 4, "The Significance of Leadership," acted on, will set some persons against others for a season. That is inevitable. A serious quest for renewal in the parish forces this issue into the open. It must be addressed concretely.

Chapter 5, "Creative Conflict," is titled precisely. Since tension and conflict are strands in the fabric of life—and change increases the intensity of both —the only issue to be determined is whether the tensions and conflicts inherent in renewal will be creative or destructive. Consequently, this chapter points up some common areas of tension and suggests several biblical and theological perspectives which can steady the controversialist. Under Christ's lordship, controversialists in the church become leaven, light, salt!

Finally, Christian readers will remember that God has liberated man in Christ. They will also remember that the cost of claiming that freedom is loyalty to the Liberator. Paul joined the historical and the existential: "God was in Christ reconciling the world to himself; therefore, be ye reconciled to God." Some are reconciled; others are not. One thief on Calvary repented; the other cursed God and died. Peter experienced new life; Judas hanged himself. Renewal occurs in the context of human freedom. Some decide *for* Christ; others decide *against* him.

## Questions for Discussion

1. What do you understand "parish renewal" to mean?

2.  Do you think renewal is a "mess" in the Protestant churches? Why?

3.  Distinguish between "tactics" and "strategy" for parish renewal. Discuss.

4.  Why did the United Presbyterian Church update its confessional position? Does your church have a "confessional" position? Do you know what your church teaches about God, Christ, the Holy Spirit, the Scriptures, the church, the state? Do you value theology?

# 1

# The Risk of Vulnerability

*If we could first know where we are, and whither we are tending, we could better judge what to do, and how to do it.*
—ABRAHAM LINCOLN

*If any man would come after me, let him deny himself and take up his cross and follow me.*

Christ humbled himself. He was born of a woman. He hungered, thirsted, wearied, wept. He was wounded for our transgressions. He was bruised for our iniquities. He suffered under Pontius Pilate, was crucified, dead, and buried. *That* was the price Jesus paid for *his* glorification. The servant is not above his Master. Each must pay the cost of renewal.

There is no diplomatic approach to renewal: "Let your yes be yes." Sentimental pleading will not bring renewal: "Get behind me, Satan." Renewal does not come by a bloodless revolution: "Put your finger here, and see my hands." New life—the daily nurture of it, the continuing need to replenish it—demands repentance and gospel faith. That makes a man vulnerable!

Shaping a ministry for renewal and keeping it flexible in the service of Christ requires the courage of candor, the rejection of pretense, the discipline of work, the resilience to absorb a thousand big and little defeats, and the willingness to suffer for the gospel. That is beyond any man. The exercise of Christ's ministry depends, therefore, on the gift of the

21

Holy Spirit. But the acceptance of that gift calls for costly discipleship. It shatters many institutional forms and reorients persons radically. To be a servant of the Word humbles the proud man, emboldens the timid man, sobers the precipitous man. That is the theme of this chapter.

I

The pastor and lay leaders must perceive the truth that the church is not a human invention but God's handiwork. The actual disposition in church circles to manage and manipulate people in the interests of an efficient institution demonstrates how shaky that conviction is in fact. Presently, this disposition is so ingrained that parish critics and secular cartoonists have had a field day! It is one reason why the world views the church simply as one social institution among many.

Let the lay leaders and the pastor examine, for example, the every-member canvass and the evangelism practices in their parish. What is the basic orientation of each: institutional security or costly witness, pressure or witness? Honest answers will cause discomfort in most parishes. Those clergy and laity who believe Jesus' promise and the apostolic witness accept the community of faith as God's idea and handiwork. Consequently, they view ministry in terms of the church's stewardship of the gospel. For them it is not "my" church, "our" church, "Pastor Smith's" church, or the "Methodist" church. It is Christ's church. Clergy and laity who take this firm position and decide practical issues with reference to it collide with fellow members who see themselves as stockholders in the corporation or as club members whose dues are paid.

The church is not simply a sociological institution. God does not intend his church to be a company of manipulated people or a cultic society directed for the esoteric satisfaction of a few. Laymen must radically change their thinking to understand and administer the local parish as a new community of one-time rebels whose treason is forgiven, whose citizenship is in the kingdom of God, whose freedom to be loyal or to rebel is unrestricted. To an unconverted mind, this seems a "messy" community. God's grace and man's freedom converge constantly to embarrass and jar the institutional church. Nonetheless, both are indispensable if the Holy Spirit is to fashion a Christian community of persons. Ecclesiastical order and institutional forms exist only to facilitate the work of the Holy Spirit. Any liturgy, dogma, polity, folk religion, or local custom which hinders the Spirit's work is the cold hand of dead tradition or the stifling weight of sentimentalism.

To challenge traditions and local practices which obscure the Word, harass the Holy Spirit, and cheapen God's grace is to risk vulnerability on many fronts. Human nature is perverse. Sincere but insecure persons frequently employ the forms of Christianity to escape God's inexorable demands, to hide from his presence.

## II

But overspiritualization, like overinstitutionalization, also weakens Christ's church. The pastor and lay leaders must perceive that the church is a human institution. The church is people—all sorts and conditions. Jesus was explicit: the wheat and the tares must be allowed to grow together. The church is an institution, a building, a corporate entity. It must be administered, its roof repaired, its articles of incorporation brought into conformity with the laws of the state. Competent personnel must be enlisted. Salaries must be paid. The corporation is liable if a citizen suffers physical injury on church premises. Since human beings are unpredictable and congregational leaders are human, the church needs discipline and order. Some lay leaders recognize this and act on it responsibly. Others find it difficult to make intelligent decisions about personnel, facilities, and salaries because they deem that sort of thing "unspiritual."

Nonetheless, institutional forms are inescapable. Man is not a disembodied spirit. He is not "a soul with ears"! He needs and devises institutional forms to communicate spirit and truth, offer love, fashion order, establish justice, and produce and distribute goods. God himself employed men and events, and finally incarnated himself in the man from Nazareth to reveal his person to man. Many laymen—and some pastors—simply do not appreciate that God-in-Christ met man "eyeball to eyeball." Christ's church is the historical means through which he continues to confront persons in time. To administer it intelligently and practically makes its leaders vulnerable to the charge that they are success-conscious institutionalists. Nonetheless, the Spirit's work will be dissipated without sound institutional forms and competent leadership. Those who lead in fashioning a flexible and sound institution open themselves to attack.

## III

The pastor and lay leaders are well advised to study some church history. Otherwise, their perspective will be limited or warped. Passion without perspective breeds confusion and causes hurt without offering healing.

The parish leaders will be steadied if they comprehend and orient to this historical perspective: however ineffectual, debased, or corrupt the church becomes, it never sinks so low that it fails to produce a remnant. Let parish pastors and lay leaders, shaken by the barrage of criticism, take heart. The parish is not likely to disappear because a band of outspoken critics predicts its demise. God is not absent from life because some people do not experience his presence. The Body of Christ, however weak or maimed, is never a dead body. The medieval church which helped to fashion feudalism did not die with the passing of feudalism. The Russian Orthodox Church, allied with the czarist suppression of the peasants and felled by the October Revolution, appears to be more vital under the Communist regime than it has been for centuries. And it is a matter of historical record that the Methodist revival in eighteenth-century England broke through the formalism of the Anglican establishment, gave a new thrust to Christ's ministry, and moved creatively into the world.

Most parishes have a residue of faith and hope and love. The leaders have the responsibility to cultivate and nurture this life in Christ, persuade others to accept it, and equip the growing remnant to witness and serve in the world. This pastoral approach—a practical expression of God's concern for persons— will make some eager parishioners impatient with their leadership, but shepherding is integral to renewal and ongoing witness. This stalwart insistence that tradition and mission go hand in hand makes the parish leaders vulnerable to criticisms from earnest social actionists.

On the other hand, the historical perspective is not altogether bright. It presents the sobering truth that the church has been and is riddled with lamentable apostasies and capitulations. Reform has been necessary in every Christian century. It is needful today. The church in modern times has deserved and received criticism. During the nineteenth century Nietzsche, Marx, and Freud launched a triple-pronged attack. That attack has not been stemmed or blunted. In the first half of the twentieth century Barth, Bultmann, Tillich, Niebuhr, and Bonhoeffer laid bare significant weaknesses in the church's life and witness. During the 1960's Bennett, Berger, Berton, Cox, Hamilton, Robinson, van Buren, and Winter made some specific criticisms which hurt because they are true, at least in part. Responsible churchmen winced; some became defensive. But many have acknowledged that the Word of the Lord *is* muted in all corners of the church by security-conscious official boards, confused parish pastors, and ecclesiastical leaders who think "institutionally." These clergy and laity are facing up to the implications of H. Richard Niebuhr's conclusion that no clear-cut conviction on the nature and purpose of the church has emerged from the parishes or theological centers.[1]

The parish leaders—ordained and lay—must indeed inquire whether the blind are leading the blind and whether the bland are counseling the bland in the congregation for which they are accountable to God. They must risk vulnerability by reassessing as they inquire into their criteria for administering the parish and into the purposes and relevance of its preaching-teaching-counseling ministry.

When the clergy and lay leaders demonstrate insight, courage, and a renewal of faith, they are in a firm position to call their fellow members to repentance and larger faith. Pretense and prejudice, ignorance and selfishness are realities in our historic churches because *they are realities in every parish.* But these evils are "the grime upon the pavement of what is still a *sacred* building: and he who would wash the pavement clean should be willing to get down on his knees to do his work inside the church."[2] When this is the posture of God's ministers, ordained and lay, the church discovers the secret of being born again. But humility makes a man vulnerable!

## IV

Since the blind cannot lead the blind, it is essential that the pastor and lay leaders recognize their own areas of blindness (limited confidence in the gospel,

[1] Niebuhr, *The Purpose of the Church and Its Ministry* (New York: Harper & Row, 1956), p. 17.

[2] A. R. Vidler, *God's Demand and Man's Response* (London: Richard's Press).

a sanguine view of sin, a careless attitude toward biblical preaching, a lethargic concern for evangelical teaching), cry *mea culpa,* repent, study, decide, act. That there is need for confession and newness of life among the parish clergy and elected lay leaders is evident from the eddies of defensiveness, defeatism, and pettiness which swirl through every parish and converge in the larger church assemblies. Envy—"sorrow at another's good fortune"—is rampant in the church as well as in the world. Jockeying for recognition, position, and power is not limited to the American corporation, the labor unions, the nation's capital, and the local country club. It is in the church, too. Openly, one is advised that a particular clergyman or layman is *persona non grata* simply because he declines to "go along to get along." The dissenter is seldom evaluated on the nature of his dissent; he is dismissed on the fact of it. Officially, the church honors prophets; actually, it is cautious, and sometimes harsh, with the few in its parishes and executive positions. Generally, official board meetings in the parish and church meetings (synod, presbytery, diocese) are perfunctory, pedantic, picayune. When it comes to "gut issues," an unspoken agreement not to disagree usually prevails. When a churchman is constrained to break that agreement and addresses an elemental issue, his colleagues explain that the difference is simply a matter of semantics, a study committee buries the issue, or the word goes out that the critic is "too individualistic." Insulation against reality is compounded. The blind glory in their blindness.

Protestant clergy and lay leaders should take Paul,

Luther, and Pope John as personal examples as well as subjects for pastoral conversation! Paul participated in an academic discussion on Mars Hill. Failing to persuade persons to decide *for* or *against* Christ in Athens, he exchanged academic argumentation for proclamation and confrontation when he reached Corinth; his subsequent impact was incalculable. Luther testified vigorously *and* indelicately to the lordship of Christ. He gave direction and impetus to a reformation which is not finished. John XXIII said essentially: "My church and I have erred and faltered in the past. We have done many things that we ought not to have done and left undone so much that God wanted done. The time has come for us to mend our ways." The world is still listening. Most liberal and conservative Protestants—and conservative Roman Catholics—have declined to speak with equal humility or candor or seriousness. Since Protestant laymen have an equal voice in official assemblies—and a majority voice in every parish—they must shoulder heavy responsibility for this disabling weakness in the contemporary church. In too many parishes laymen pressure, harass, and reject clergy and fellow laymen who dare to witness boldly. In others, they actually foster blandness.

Another weakness in the church stems from parish pastors and lay officials who entertain the notion that they alone face radical social change in a revolutionary world. In most parishes and general church meetings the discussion centers on the revolutionary changes in the world and the ineffectiveness of the congregation; there is little evidence that the assembly of leaders has real confidence in the gospel of God. They focus on the problem rather than on the saving power of Christ. Scientists, educators, businessmen, political leaders, and parents are also wrestling with the dynamics of unprecedented social change. The unwillingness of some churchmen to recognize this suggests that their confidence in the gospel is situationally qualified.

An intellectually convinced, emotionally resilient, committed leadership is indispensable to church renewal. Those who like to manage the institution and those who "enjoy" church activities are not able to trumpet the news that Christ is the "man for all seasons." Until *these* parish leaders expose their persons for the sake of the gospel, they short-circuit renewal. They are part of the problem. Conviction and committees are not mutually exclusive, but the Bible must take priority over *Robert's Rules of Order!* There is a time for proclamation and a time for dialogue. There is a place for confrontation and a place for negotiation. There is a season for intercessory prayer and a season for prophetic speech. The bland cannot lead the bland. Personal *and* institutional vulnerability—for Christ—must be risked.

## V

Parish renewal calls for the clear-eyed recognition that theological and practical correctives must be viewed as *correctives,* not as substantive solutions. The current emphasis on the "involved" God (God immanent) must not obscure the transcendent God.[3] Man and society need the holy, sovereign God as well

[3] Dietrich Bonhoeffer, *Letters and Papers from Prison* (New York: The Macmillan Company, 1953).

as the suffering servant. Equally, the current war on
"cheap grace" must not obscure the reality of grace
itself. Preaching and teaching the demands of Christ
apart from his promises caricatures the gospel. Ethical
instruction, separated from the kerygma, may appeal
to social gospelers, but it is *not* the gospel.[4] The
doctrine of the two kingdoms—summarily dismissed
by some contemporary theologians—is essential in the
work of Christ's church; the secular city and the Kingdom of God are not interchangeable.[5] Initially, the
burden of responsibility for surefootedness on these
issues rests with the pastor. If he shrugs it off saying,
"I'm no theologian," the lay leaders must recall him
to his duty, challenge him by asking serious questions,
and encourage him to search the theological minds in
this and other centuries. And that will make the
whole parish vulnerable.

The "practical" correctives also present a deceptive
trap. Alert parish pastors will resist the how-to-do-it
books which suggest that parish renewal can be had
by some special approach or method—Bible study
groups, a downtown counseling center, a coffee house,
a lay academy, Bible preaching, a sound educational
program, an evangelism program, a jazz liturgy, *et al*.
These are *tactics* for parish renewal and ongoing
witness. Any one or all of them can be useful. That
depends on the situation and the cultural climate.
But there is only one strategy: the objective-subjec-

----

[4] J. A. T. Robinson, *Honest to God* (Philadelphia: The
Westminster Press, 1961), esp. pp. 122-41.

[5] Gerhard Ebeling, *Word and Faith* (Philadelphia: Fortress
Press, 1964), pp. 386-406, presents "the necessity" for the doctrine. Harvey Cox, *The Secular City* (New York: The Macmillan Company, 1965), pp. 107-8, dismisses the doctrine.

tive proclamation of God's Word of judgment and grace must make it clear that God speaks relevantly to the human condition.[6] In the presence of the Living Word, some persons in their freedom accept and others reject Christ. Responsible clergy challenge—and resist if necessary—excited laymen who, fresh from a district conference on renewal, shout, "Eureka, we've found the program for renewal!" Simplistic solutions are no more valid in the parish than in the political arena. There is increasing risk to those who stand firm on this issue, because new forms are now equated with renewal itself—"the medium is the message."

Further, to view the parish as a mission field—which it is—must not produce a leadership which sets out to convert "church members" for ten years before it calls them to witness "in the world." *Laymen live in the world,* and that, obviously, is the *only* place to exercise Christ's ministry. The church witnesses in word and deed to challenge the comfortable residents of the world and to enlighten and support the uneasy residents, enabling anyone who chooses Christ to march to another drumbeat. The fact that most church members are biblically illiterate and theologically naïve, and that many are uninformed or prejudiced on sociopolitical issues, must not obscure the biblical distinction between conversion and growth in grace. It is the church's task to *convert* persons to Christ; equally, the church has the responsibility to *enlighten, nurture,* and *equip* these converts so they

---

[6] This will be considered in chapter 2. For a full discussion and application see *Preaching and Parish Renewal,* Part I; and *From Tradition to Mission,* chaps. 4, 5, and 6.

can witness and serve where they live and work and play. The parish church is the center of worship and learning and pastoral care where the Word of God persuades, motivates, and equips persons to witness in the world, to test the doctrine for themselves, and to say a good word for Christ *now*.

Until each parish accepts its responsibility to speak for God in and to the world, however falteringly, his Word may not be spoken in that community. If this silence is compounded from parish to parish, the institutional church as we know it will perish as a finite social institution in a perishing finite culture, and God's work will go on in other places through other persons.[7] It is the love of Christ which constrains the church to address persons, confront power structures in the community, and shape the public mind wherever it can. Reconciliation, biblically viewed, is a rugged affair. It comes by way of the Cross. To follow Christ into the world requires that the clergy and lay officers obey his commandments. The commotion, tension, and conflict engendered by this disciplined Christian witness is as severe in a religionized situation as it is in a pagan setting. Secularists can be harsh; religionists can be vicious. Hearing and doing the truth, every Christian's proper response to God, makes a man vulnerable in the parish *and* the community in any generation.

## VI

The pastor and lay leaders must recognize the need for renewal in their congregation. Decisions must be

[7] A trenchant observation which Paul Tillich made several decades ago.

made and implemented in one's own congregation. It is easier to read and talk about parish renewal at church council meetings or in hospitable study groups than to face the need for it in the congregation's Sunday school, parish organizations, and worship services. Addressing the need concretely in these and related areas of parish life requires painstaking study, careful listening to people who disagree, candor, compassion, courage, and patience. It is exhausting to identify the attitudes, practices, and traditions which block renewal in a particular parish—an antiquated constitution, a niggardly budget, veneration for the Bible as an object of faith, an unhealthy affection for a liturgy which speaks only to a particular in-group. But concrete identifications must be made from *the pulpit* (pastoral leadership) and in every corner of the parish by the pastor *and* the lay officers (corporate leadership). Renewal is an invigorating process which calls for specific diagnoses, particular identifications, personal confrontations, concrete decisions, and personal travail. But it keeps one vulnerable in every corner of the parish.

Obviously, renewal in each congregation must begin *somewhere*. Unless it begins at the top, it is not likely to begin anywhere. An indecisive leadership is worse than no leadership at all. The parish leaders must be motivated to accept their responsibility to do and to be, by God's grace, what the gospel requires of every Christian. Otherwise, their impact on the membership will be negligible. But the cost is high—and personal. The tensions and conflicts engendered by these naked encounters with the Word produce antagonism and alienation in the official board and among the members. The way of the Cross is too hard for many. It always has been. But wherever members are learning to love Christ rather than their own egos and to value persons above programs, new life will stir that parish. And this new life in the congregation matures across the years so long as it is nurtured from the Word *and* demonstrated in the clerical and lay leadership.

The primary need is for clergy, lay leaders, and the general membership to come under the Word of the Lord in judgment and grace so that the Holy Spirit can call, persuade, and enlighten persons who, in their freedom, respond. Each member decides for himself whether he will take up Christ's ministry. Renewal does not come by efficient management of the institution or by clever manipulation of members. Neither does it come through change for the sake of change. Tradition and mission go hand in hand.

## VII  1499327

Finally, because the image of ministry entertained and projected by pastors and people affects radically the degree to which the church exercises Christ's ministry, it is imperative that they discern the authentic image and orient to it. That task makes churchmen vulnerable in their institutional life and in a religionized culture.

The quest for an authentic image does not begin within the context of the profession or the denominational structure; it begins within the context of the Faith. Standing humbly before the tribunal of biblical evidence, pastor and people discover that the authentic minister (ordained and lay) is a man—

perverse, finite, lost. Justified through faith, made new in Christ, he is still a man. The Christian is not a holy man; he is a servant of the holy God. The Holy Spirit persuades and enables this new creature, obedient in his freedom, to communicate the living Word through his freedom. This witness, herald, steward, shepherd, prophet—grateful that he is cared for by Christ—cares for others from Christ's love, confronting them with God's demands and promises and equipping them from the Word to be prophets, teachers, and evangelists where they live.

## Questions for Discussion

1. Examine the biblical bases for calling Christian discipleship "costly." Apply them to your parish situation.

2. What place does personal conversion and growth in grace have in parish renewal?

3. What relationship exists between parish renewal and (a) Bible study? (b) theological inquiry and dialogue? (c) prophetic preaching? (d) social action? (e) social ministry? (f) confession and intercessory prayer?

4. Are tradition and mission mutually exclusive in the renewal of the parish? Be specific about *your* parish in the perspective of church history.

5. Distinguish between a corrective and a substantive solution in parish renewal.

6. What is the essential nature of authentic ministry? To what degree do *you* judge it to exist in and through your parish?

7. What are the particular points of vulnerability for the renewalist in your parish?

# 2

# By Whose Authority?

*Every true renewal of the Church is based on hearing anew of the Word of God as it comes to us in the Bible.*
—W. A. VISSER 'T HOOFT

*It is Lambeth's duty to remind Westminster that Westminster is responsible to God.*
—WILLIAM TEMPLE, THE LATE ARCHBISHOP OF CANTERBURY

In three action-packed centuries the American conquered a wilderness, settled a continent, and fashioned his own civilization. In that complex process he proved that he loves freedom for himself and, under inner and external constraint, will provide or safeguard it for others. During the first two thirds of the twentieth century the American fought a war "to make the world safe for democracy"; provided the muscle to stop the totalitarian onslaught of the Nazis and the Japanese expansionists; led in establishing a world organization of nations; expended billions of dollars to rebuild western Europe; and contained Communism in Greece, Berlin, Korea, and Cuba. During the 1930's and the 1960's this same American also engineered within the framework of the law the two most intensive and extensive social revolutions in single decades of recorded history.

The American loves freedom; that is written indelibly into history. But he dislikes discipline. He questions any authority which limits his freedom unless he can see that it benefits him directly. The American—individualistic, idealistic, experimental, pragmatic, inventive—reacts immaturely to authority: "Oh Yeah!" "Who says so?" "Nobody tells me what to do." Three perceptive, sympathetic European historians—de Tocqueville, Bryce, Brogan—assessing the American mind at half-century intervals, documented this temper of mind. Henry Steele Commager, appraising the American at mid-twentieth century, states flatly: "Two world wars had not induced in him either a sense of sin or that awareness of evil almost instinctive with most Old World peoples. . . . War had not taught him discipline or respect for authority." [1]

The man in the American pew also loves freedom; but he too is undisciplined, indisposed to accept authority. He has a dull sense of sin and little awareness of evil as a deep-seated reality in life. This is the lay leader in the American parish. This is the ordained clergyman in many places. All people, of course, want freedom without discipline; that is human nature. But our tradition of anti-authoritarian individualism dulls the American's sensitivity to the serious nature of this human disability. Most Americans are not prone to accept any external standard of judgment upon their persons, ideas, actions. When an ecumenical conclave calls the church to acknowledge that Christ is Lord, American churchmen respond affirmatively. But when these same churchmen get down to examine what Christ's lordship requires in their parish, the storm clouds gather. When they recognize

[1] *The American Mind* (New Haven: Yale University Press, 1959), p. 410.

that the Lord of the church collides with them over *their* money, politics, business goals, and social customs, the storm breaks with fury. Until God's authority is recognized and acknowledged *in the parish,* renewal is a theme for books and articles, a word to be savored, an idea to be discussed, a concept to be examined, but not a reality experienced in that congregation.

Theologically, Protestants agree on the seat of authority: *sola scriptura.* That, they exclaim, is why the Reformation surged out of Geneva and Wittenberg. Theoretically, Protestants understand why their Roman Catholic brethren are engulfed presently by waves of controversy over the question of authority: scripture and/or tradition. Both Protestants and Roman Catholics know that pre-Reformation councils faced that question, backed away, and schism resulted. They know that the Reformers decided that Scripture is the primary authority. But the authority of Scripture is now blurred for most Protestants. At the grass roots they face a dilemma on three levels: the dead hand of particular denominational-sectarian traditions, the relationship between the Scriptures and the Word of God, and the interpretation of the Scriptures' witness to God's mighty deeds.

In the complex aftermath of the Reformation, separate groups (Lutherans, Calvinists, Mennonites), having accepted the Scriptures as their rule of faith, proceeded to develop traditions peculiar to themselves (polity, liturgy, dogma, ethics). These differences, a major characteristic of American church life, are a barrier to renewal in the parish. Some conflicting Protestant traditions root in national origins, the

American frontier experience, and local mores. A source of conflict more elemental than any of these is the lack of agreement on the nature and interpretation of the Scriptures and their authority. One is right to declare, "United Presbyterians believe . . ." Christian dialogue is best served when persons speak from one Christian tradition to another, from faith to faith. But it is essential, if the dialogue is to be liberating and creative, that each tradition join other traditions in a mutual examination of the particular doctrines of each before the tribunal of biblical evidence.

Some Lutherans prize their liturgy more than they value their church's doctrine of the Word of God; and others, able to quote a bit from Luther's Small Catechism, know nothing of the eschatological thrust in the book of Revelation. Some Methodists, abrasively moralistic, exhibit little of the evangelicalism of John Wesley; others, quick to form evangelism committees, exhibit little of George Whitefield's evangelistic fervor. Some Episcopalians, wedded to the *Book of Common Prayer,* demonstrate through divisions between and within their House of Bishops and House of Deputies (on theological and sociopolitical issues) a lack of unanimity on the authority of the Scriptures. United Presbyterians also wrestle with this crucial issue, a vocal minority among them having taken public exception to their church's confession of 1967, a modern supplement to its historic statement of faith (the Westminster Confession of 1647). The United Church of Christ, born in 1957 at a cost of three hundred Congregational Churches which remained aloof on "traditional" grounds, is far from being agreed on what the Scriptures say to them.[2]

The self-acknowledged conservative churches (and sects) are getting into deep water too. This vigorous wing of Protestantism has begun to look critically at its dated traditions. Its younger clergy are examining the Scriptures in the light of biblical scholarship, and a segment of its laity is engaging in daring acts of social service and bold protest. Controversy seethes beneath the surface in the once placid gatherings of the conservatives. Baptists, United Brethren, Mennonites, one body of Lutherans—and scores more— are experiencing presently the travail which Methodists, Episcopalians, United Presbyterians, the United Church of Christ, and a branch of Lutherans (LCA) experienced in their theological schools several decades ago. But few clergymen in *these* churches have encouraged the general membership to face the implications of an accepted biblical scholarship. Until that happens parish by parish, renewal will not sweep the church. An unread Bible should not concern the church more than a misread Bible. The parishioner's "I believe . . ." or "I think . . ." must evidence his acceptance of the authority of God's Word. Presently that is not the case.

Culturally and historically the American parish appears to be the last refuge of unbridled individualism. Here a man who feels frustrated and cramped by the external disciplines of his family, his job, or his citizenship feels free to exercise unrestrained authority.

[2] The United Church of Christ is a result of the 1957 merger of the Evangelical and Reformed Church and the Congregational Christian Churches.

The priesthood of believers is distorted into an every-man-his-own-boss doctrine. In many parishes this individual authoritarianism is a major barrier to renewal.

The man who feels unrewarded and unrecognized on his job becomes the authoritarian voice in the church council. The woman bound by an unhappy marriage and several recalcitrant teen-agers regards the Ladies' Aid as her private empire. Nor is the clergyman immune from this cultural strand which is hospitable to sin. Many a pastor nurtures a clique within the parish who love him and feed his unfilled ego. The Word of God is handled not as an authoritative Word from a sovereign Lord, but as a crutch for insecure persons or as a platform on which empty men and women can rise to positions of power and prestige in the little world of their parish. Emotionally undisciplined church people, ordained and lay, can and do use the Word as a blunt instrument to bludgeon those who differ from them doctrinally and morally and, too often of late, economically and politically.

Each parish, therefore, must wrestle concretely with the question of authority. What authority, if any, is respected in one's parish? What authority resides in the office of the pastor, the bishop, the elected lay leaders? Are these persons functionaries and are they subject to a higher authority? These questions call for serious biblical and theological study among the laity. Is authority in one's parish resident in several substantial contributors or in a cadre of respected senior members? An honest answer to that question will bring pain and, if acted on, possibly a reduced budget. Does authority reside in the institution's traditional structures? Addressing that question will be irksome for alert members and distasteful to those who like things as they are.

The first issue to be decided, then, in any parish is whether its clerical and lay leaders will accept the authority of God or man. No parish can serve two masters. A parish divided against itself must fall. Renewal in any congregation and its maturing witness to Christ depend on whether the decision to honor God is made firmly in the light of Scripture and held tenaciously in faith. Only as the members are confronted in their freedom with the demands and promises of God will some be motivated and equipped by the Holy Spirit to proclaim and demonstrate Christ's victory in the world. This means that the parish leaders, especially the clergy, must accept the authority of God and mediate it through a ministry faithful to his Word. The primary need is for the parish leaders to decide whether *they* will accept the authority of God or man. That decision is made properly before the tribunal of biblical evidence. It is renewed there daily.

But how shall evidence be taken before that tribunal? Who rules on the evidence? In what sense, substance or form, is Scripture inspired? Is the Bible the Word of God or does it contain the Word of God? What is the relation between the Word of God and the words of men? If God's self-revelation is progressive—and the record demonstrates that it is—how can all Scripture be of equal authority? Since Christ is the full expression of God's self-revelation in history, is he not the only sure guide for interpreting all Scripture?

A brief account of Protestantism's chasmic differences in approaching the Bible will provide perspective. During the seventeenth and eighteenth centuries most Protestants reacted fiercely to the arrogant authoritarianism of the papacy and the absolutist authoritarianism of kings by insisting that there was only *one* ultimate authority, the Bible—infallible, inerrant, dictated word for word by God himself. During the nineteenth century European biblical scholars demonstrated the historical untenability of that position. Their studies precipitated liberalism in the twentieth-century church. These enlightened, optimistic churchmen softened the Scriptures' firm witness on the nature of God and man. They proved to be more intellectual than biblical or existential. Meanwhile, the seventeenth-century tradition of literalism continued to inform fundamentalism which hardened Scripture into a set of divine truths. Its champions viewed sin and grace, faith and new life, mechanically; they were anti-intellectual, rarely existential; they treated the Bible as a "Paper Pope." Evangelical fundamentalists like Campbell Morgan were exceptions who proved the rule.

The collisions between the modernists and fundamentalists four decades ago were violent. The unsavory details of that intense, acrimonious, mean-spirited struggle between the representatives of the two views cannot concern us here.[3] But the *issue* at stake in that struggle must concern us; it is not

[3] See, for example, the autobiography of Harry Emerson Fosdick, *The Living of These Days: An Autobiography* (New York: Harper & Row, 1956). See also Richard Hofstadter, *Anti-Intellectualism in American Life* (New York: Alfred A. Knopf, 1963).

dead. It is very much alive in fundamentalist churches and for many laymen in the "confessional" churches. This widespread confusion and elemental conflict over biblical interpretation must be faced and addressed creatively in each parish if renewal is to invigorate the membership. It is not enough to declare that renewal "is based on hearing anew of the Word of God as it comes to us in the Bible." Agreement must be reached on how to discern the living Word in the Scriptures and how it confronts contemporary man. Biblical scholarship exists to aid the church in preaching and teaching the Word.

Many Protestant laymen today are biblical illiterates, biblical mechanics, or do-it-yourself demythologizers.[4] Too often the clergy—exhausted by keeping the institutional wheels turning, faltering under an "office" demeaned by petty expectations, pressured to preach innocuous homilies—have softened the radical biblical insights, avoided doctrinal preaching, and substituted "church" chatter for serious theological conversation. The results are painfully evident. American churchmen treat Jesus with respect but avoid personal involvement with him. They ignore the Bible as irrelevant or venerate it as an object of faith. They emasculate the historical Jesus and sentimentalize the objective gospel. God's Word has objective reality; it means more than any subjective piety reads into it. And it certainly has a relevance which pragmatism fails to grasp. The enemy within

[4] Later in this discussion I shall examine demythologization. Here the term is used loosely to include intellectuals who strip away "the world view" of the biblical writers; rationalists who strip away what they judge to be irrational; and a majority of laymen who accept what suits their fancy.

the church may be more dangerous than the enemy without.

Biblical scholarship, having cleared the air in most theological schools, must be brought into the parish through the pulpit (catechetical sermons), classroom (methodology and content), and small groups (dialogue and application) so that serious laymen can be enlightened and equipped to read Scripture meaningfully. Unless the parish clergy accept this responsibility, Jesus will be imprisoned in a book or lost in the mists of value judgments which reflect one's culture. We are not implying that biblical scholarship offers a magical formula for renewal. It does not. It exists to enable the church to preach and teach the Word effectively. It is a tool which must be employed to set before persons the fundamentals of the faith, especially *the* fundamental: "God was in Christ reconciling the world to himself." Biblical scholarship exists to define the context in which God's mightiest deed was accomplished: "Many were the forms and fashions in which God spoke of old to our fathers." Biblical scholarship serves a constructive purpose when it helps laymen to discern the Word of God in the words of men. But it must be employed at the parish level. This summary statement will serve here.

A half-century ago Karl Barth's liberal theological stance was shaken by World War I (a fight to the finish between "Christian" nations). Convinced that the liberals had been too optimistic and man-centered, Barth rejected liberalism and set out to recover the Word of God *in Scripture* as the only authority for preaching and teaching. His central aim was to recover the Word as objective reality and to put God at the center. Pointing vigorously to the gulf between God and man, Barth argued that man, not God, is lost. Man cannot "find" God; God-in-Christ finds man. The record of that event is in the Bible. The Swiss theologian, having rejected liberalism, proceeded to attack fundamentalism for treating the Bible as a "self-sufficient Paper Pope." Overreacting against liberalism, Barth stated flatly that God is not revealed in nature or history. Overreacting against fundamentalism, the crisis theologian insisted that the Word of God cannot be identified with the words of the Bible. Unintentionally, therefore, Barth opened the way for radical demythologization in the next generation. Luther and Paul would have recognized immediately—as Barth's contemporaries eventually did—that his influential theology was, at some points, "out of this world"!

Although serious Bible scholars had been demythologizing for years—and the use of myth had long been recognized in presenting the story of the Creation and the Fall—it was the German scholar Rudolf Bultmann who, addressing the New Testament, went at the task with vigor. Bultmann's challenge to all Christian teachers may prove to be his most significant contribution. "They must make it quite clear what their hearers are expected to accept and what they are not. At all costs the preacher must not leave his people in the dark about what he secretly eliminates, nor must he be in the dark about it himself." [5] It is significant to remember that Bultmann began with the practical problem of biblical preaching.

[5] H. W. Bartsch, ed., *Kerygma and Myth* (Torchbook ed.; New York: Harper & Row, 1961), p. 9.

Because the word "myth" looms large in the controversy over Bultmann's methodology (hermeneutics),
we shall describe simply how it is understood in biblical and theological circles. "Myth" is not synonymous
with "fairy tale." It is a literary form which its em-
ployer does not expect to be taken literally; he uses it
to point to a truth which he cannot express in any
other form. Fundamentalists view all myth (Creation,
Fall) as history. Liberals view all myth as folk tales.
Neo-orthodoxists view myth as a literary form which
communicates God's truth. For example, Reinhold
Niebuhr, whose penetrating analysis of the origin
and nature of sin roots in the biblical view of man,
treats the Fall with intense seriousness. But like Tillich, he views Christ's resurrection symbolically.
Nearly all Christian laymen practice some demythologization; we cannot dismiss Bultmann with a casual
word. Courageously, he applied the principle fully
to the New Testament.

Bultmann's argument, stripped to the core, is that
the gospel as first delivered in the New Testament
was conceived and presented mythologically. The
Gospels are not biographies of Jesus; they are evangelistic tracts which employ the thought patterns of
that day. Consequently, modern man, who thinks
and communicates differently, cannot possibly understand the Christian message unless it is demythol-
ogized. Specifically, Bultmann means that the gospel
must be interpreted existentially. He interprets traditional language in his own way. He classifies Jesus'
birth, death, and resurrection as mythological. He
contends that the historical Jesus is lost in the midst
of the centuries. Jesus is not datable; we cannot know

him as he was in the flesh. Consequently, Bultmann raises fundamental questions. How does the Christian understand history? What is the relation between the Word of God and the words of men? On what foundation does the Faith rest? How can one be sure of Christ?

Demythologizers, and symbolists such as Paul Tillich, argue that modern science has removed the ground for a legitimate faith in the supernatural world. Certainly the Newtonian universe is gone and the mechanical god which its devotees created is dead; but the judgment that the new science destroys the ground for any belief in a supernatural world is too sweeping to accept uncritically. The church must appraise that view carefully. William James's "will to believe" is a poor response in this age of scientism, but the efforts of Karl Heim and Pierre Teilhard de Chardin are suggestive.[6]

The demythologizers and the symbolists, having stirred the scholars of Christendom, are now getting a substantial hearing outside the cloistered halls of the theological schools. In England, John A. T. Robinson (*Honest to God*) popularized some of Bultmann and Bonhoeffer, misinterpreting the latter. Pierre Berton (*The Comfortable Pew*) qualifies as Canada's "lay Robinson." Both men, Robinson and Berton, have received a wide hearing in this country. The "God is dead" writers, naming Paul Tillich as their spiritual

[6] Heim, *God and Science* (New York: Harper & Bros., 1953); and Teilhard de Chardin, *The Future of Man* (Harper & Row, 1964) can prod churchmen to fashion a meaningful "natural theology."

father, have popularized some of his insights.[7] Paul
van Buren, linguistic analyst, proposes that the traditional religious semantics are dead. Thomas J. J.
Altizer points dramatically to what he calls the fact of
God's death in our time. William Hamilton attempts
to explicate for our day some of the obscure insights
included in the prison witness of Bonhoeffer; namely,
that in a religionless commitment to Christ we have
freedom to follow him in being "the man for others."

There is uneven value in these contemporary efforts
to devise relevant means for proclaiming the gospel,
but there *is* value. Van Buren's call to reexamine
traditional religious language is helpful. Altizer's con-
tention that God is dead because the Christian tradition is meaningless in contemporary history prods
serious churchmen to ask whether the Word is
present in traditional church forms. Bultmann's
insistence that Jesus provided no system of values and
rules "intelligible for all men" is a biblical truth which
American parishioners need to learn and honor.[8] Tillich's view that "love can never become fanatical in a
fight for the absolute or cynical under the impact of
the relative" is an essential theological insight for
churchmen everywhere.[9] Bultmann and Tillich—
like other serious scholars who were and are eager to
proclaim the gospel relevantly—present a two-

[7] In the sense that Tillich, seeking to abolish God as an
*idol* in the traditional churchman's mind, insisted that God does
not exist (that is, he is not dependent on anything outside his
own person), the eminent philosopher-theologian sired these men.

[8] Bultmann, *Jesus and the Word* (New York: Charles Scribner's Sons, 1961), p. 84.

[9] Tillich, *Systematic Theology* (Chicago: University of Chicago Press, 1951), I, 152.

pronged challenge to Protestantism. They expose its lack of candor and its deep-seated anti-intellectualism. The church needs its avant-garde as well as its rear guard!

But the challenge posed by the avant-garde is packaged dangerously. The methodology of the demythologizers and symbolists undercuts the historical foundations of the Christian faith. They are the new "subjectivists." They offer significant insights and deserve to be studied critically but, in their extremity, they must be rejected. The existentialist approach to Scripture and theology rests on a half-truth and is, therefore, deceptively dangerous. Kierkegaard's "leap of faith" is only partially true. It is a matter of record that God *did* raise Jesus from the dead! If that liberating news could not be authenticated historically, it would be wicked to urge anyone to leap. Each man's leap is existential; the ground for making it is historical. Peter put it succinctly: "We did not follow cleverly devised myths." Because God was in the historical Jesus, Paul could urge men to accept him. Fact and value, history and faith, are inextricably bound up in Christian revelation. Value is abstract apart from fact. Christian faith is meaningless outside the context of human history. God speaks to us through the words of men. In one sense, therefore, Bultmann and Tillich are as subjective as the nineteenth-century liberals were. The Christian kerygma cannot be separated altogether from myth. The New Testament writers used it partly because of their subject matter. The elements of myth have unique meaning when viewed in the light of the historical Jesus. The Gospels are not biographies, but they do present the historical ground on which a man meets God in the flesh. Jesus is datable and knowable. The church asks no one to accept Christ on blind faith; the evidence is objective.

Ebeling points out that the problems arising out of our contemporary situation cannot be solved by modernizing our vocabulary, for that is simply to treat external symptoms. He inquires pointedly: "Has preaching lost its authority because the word 'God' has become unintelligible, or has the word 'God' become an empty term because preaching turned empty?" In a world fragmented, disordered, and confused by a babel of authoritarian voices, "our talk of God must secure for itself the recognition which it claims." That is precisely what the Word does by addressing man in his elemental situation.

The basic situation of man cannot be regarded in abstraction, in separation from the concretions beneath which it is concealed, ignored, or forgotten. On the contrary, the word of God brings this basic situation to expression precisely in its concretions. That is why the language of the Bible is so rich and so close to reality. This is felt even by those who do not perceive the word of God in the Bible. Above all, however, that this is the Bible's way of speaking results in the fact that the announcement of what is hidden takes place not as theoretic enlightenment or as an appeal for the realization of an ideal, but in such a way that man is transposed into his basic situation as word situation. The Bible's way of saying this is to place man before God; that is to say, the word of God alters the situation decisively. It does so by placing man in a concrete word situation; it does so through a word of faith that testifies to love and therefore awakens hope. This is why the word of God is uttered historically and is inseparable from narrative, appearing in its fullness as man, as the man Jesus. To believe in him means to be transposed in him into our own basic situation. This is no artificial substitute, but a promising fulfillment. For the truth that makes man true lies outside himself—that is his basic situation.[10]

The threat from the right, fundamentalism, is as dangerous, finally, as the threat from the left. This approach to the Scriptures flattens the Bible, placing its sixty-six books on the same level, rather than putting God-in-Christ at the center of biblical study. The Song of Solomon, for example, is placed on an equal footing with the Gospel of John.[11] This approach, inherited from the seventeenth century, constitutes a harsh attack on the Bible in our day because it offends enlightened minds and alienates sensitive spirits.

Described simply, fundamentalism incorporates literalism, moralism, and rigorous attacks on any scholarship which contradicts a literal biblical text. Intellectually sophisticated fundamentalists accept and engage in scholarly addressments to the Scriptures, but they maintain rigidly—without historical evidence—that the original text, forever lost, was inerrant in all details. The fundamentalist view dominates the conservative churches and the sects, but it also flourishes in the confessional churches. Talking at, back to, and about one another in Christian circles

[10] Ebeling, *God and Word*, p. 45.
[11] Some enlightened fundamentalists do not commit this particular error, but the majority do.

is a luxury which the church cannot afford in this revolutionary era. Conversations *and* confrontations must occur in parish after parish, since churchmen of all stripes live and work together *there*.

The Bible must be protected from its existentialist friends—the demythologizers and symbolists. It must be rescued from its fundamentalist defenders—the literalists and moralists. The former would lose Christ and his message in the mists of value and symbols. The latter would imprison him in a book and devalue his message. The Bible must be freed to speak its sovereign message to a needy and waiting world: God-in-Christ saves any lost person who responds in faith and obedience. That is the good news which laymen need to hear, understand, proclaim, and teach. But it cannot be communicated apart from responsible and enlightened Bible study in the parish.

Christ and the Bible are inseparable. Christians believe in the Bible because of Christ; they also believe in Christ because of the Bible. But they acknowledge Christ's lordship over all Scripture. In Scripture man is confronted with God's mighty deeds, especially his decisive act in Christ. But Jesus is not to be separated from the whole biblical faith in God the Creator (human family), the God of history (chosen people), the God of the church (people of God), and the God of final judgment (victory for his kingdom). This view rescues Scripture from the mists of existentialism and liberates it from a literalistic prison because it accepts history and faith, facts and values. This view is historical and existential. It is objective and subjective. Jesus is neither a phantom nor a contemporary prophet.

Once we acknowledge that the Bible is the inspired human record of God's progressive self-revelation and that it must be interpreted with Christ as the guide, we can face the historical fact that the Old Testament writers borrowed heavily from other ancient religions (the Flood). We can recognize that myth is employed to communicate God's cosmic deed (Creation) and man's irrational choice (the Fall). We can also accept legend (David and Goliath) and drama (Job) as human media through which God speaks. We can recognize that the prophetic message in the Old Testament, while clear in its promise of Christ, is valued not simply as an oracular thrust into a "future" we now know, but as an onrushing witness to God's unbroken presence (judgment and mercy) in human experience, coming to full expression in Jesus Christ and continuing in history through the fellowship of those who accept the Resurrection Christ. The sovereign, righteous, omnipotent God of the Israelites is the patient, merciful, suffering servant (Isaiah 53) whom the church knows, serves, and proclaims as Christ. That is the Scriptures' testimony: God liberates man through Christ's deed.

The staggering truth that God loves all men exactly as they are, wherever they are, in whatever condition they are outflanks the most versatile imagination. It is too big to capture. The best theologies falter under the grandeur of it. The most persuasive preaching falls short in proclaiming it. Christian hymnody reaches for it magnificently: "There's a wideness in God's mercy, Like the wideness of the sea"; and again, "To those who fall how kind thou art, how good to those who seek." But only the Scriptures capture both fact and spirit: "God so loved the world that he gave . . ." So loved! That is the dominant theme in the Scriptures' witness from creation to redemption. God so loved that he gave his only Son. That is the good news, the message of liberation. God was in Christ! That event is the focal point in the Scriptures' witness to God's mighty acts. Christ is the *only* sure interpreter of Scripture.

But it is possible, even with Christ as guide, to ignore his vibrant person and read the New Testament mechanically and the Old Testament narrowly. This approach ignores the significance of God's *progressive* self-revelation in human history. It robs Scripture of its depth dimension. Scripture is not "bigger than life"; it is life. It is human experience (history) with God in the center of it. To read Jonah in the shadow of the Cross, to study Hosea in the context of Jesus' pastoral concern for the woman taken in adultery, to meditate on the Cross from the perspective of Isaiah's suffering servant, is to hear God speak *now* for it is to hear how he spoke *then*. Christ—not man nor an institution—is the rightful interpreter of the Scriptures, for "God acted as he did in Old Testament days just because he would, in the fullness of time, do what he did through Christ." [12]

This does not mean that the Word of God is limited to the words of men or even to the words of Jesus which are recorded in the New Testament. The mind of Lincoln is not limited to the words of Sandburg in

[12] Anders Nygren, *The Significance of the Bible for the Church,* trans. C. C. Rasmussen (Philadelphia: Fortress Press, 1964), p. 14.

his insightful study or even to the words of Lincoln himself at Gettysburg. Edgar J. Goodspeed points out that the recorded words of Jesus, if spoken consecutively, would run less than two hours. "How little of his teaching has been preserved! Yet that little was so stirring, so moving and so penetrating that it is safe to say nobody else has influenced the world so much. But think of it! To be able to say in two hours enough to change the current of mankind!" [13] Nonetheless, Jesus' revelation of God is more than the thirty or so recorded parables, the Eleventh Commandment, the Golden Rule, and the Sermon on the Mount. Luther is helpful in suggesting that we begin with the sayings of Jesus, but he does not suggest that these sayings are the whole Word of God to man. The Word of God is *all* that Jesus said, did, was, is. It encompasses his words and acts, life and death, resurrection and abiding presence. Christ is God's Word but, says Luther, "Scripture begins tenderly and leads us to Christ as a man, then to the Lord over all creatures, and then to God." [14]

Biblically viewed, the Word of God is the good news of God's saving work in Christ—the message about the essential nature and purpose of God in every evidence of his dynamic, saving activity, initiated at creation and revealed progressively at his own pace through myth, legend, historical events, historical persons (Amos, Hosea, John the Baptist), and preeminently in the historical person of his Son, Jesus

[13] Goodspeed, *A Life of Jesus* (New York: Harper & Row, 1950), p. 76.

[14] Joseph Sittler, *The Doctrine of the Word* (Philadelphia: Board of Publication, ULCA, 1948), p. 7.

Christ. That revelation is dynamic, not static. The Bible "is both the message of that action and its continuation." [15] The church accepts Scripture as the inspired but uneven witness to God's saving activity. "Revelation is not a thing; it is a continuing activivity." [16] "If the Scriptures themselves, as a whole, claim to be the Word of God, they can be this only if they are, as a whole, interpreted in terms of Christ. . . . Christ is Lord of the Scriptures." [17] This report of God's saving activity is more than a report; and the Christ event, rooted in a precise moment of history, is not bound by history. The message of Christ, as Luther observed, "is to me not simply an old song about an event that happened 1500 years ago . . . ; it is a gift and bestowing that endures forever." That incorporates magnificently the historical and the existential. Revelation is—and continues to be—a decisive intervention of God in the affairs of men. Wherever a community of people accepts the living Word and shares it through preaching, teaching, and the administration of the sacraments, Christ confronts persons as he did in Galilee.

The Bible is a collection of writings, sixty-six books in all, which differ in theme, background, and authorship. It is the rich, varied, human, inspired record—employing myth, legend, and parable, historical events, historical persons and the historical Jesus—

---

[15] Nygren, *The Significance of the Bible for the Church*, p. 4.

[16] Sittler, *The Doctrine of the Word*, p. 11.

[17] Martin Luther. Quoted in an unpublished lecture, "Word of God, Sacraments, and Ministry," by T. G. Tappert, professor of church history, Lutheran Theological Seminary at Philadelphia.

of God's saving activity. Paul and Luther recognized the unity between the old and the new covenants because they perceived the unity in revelation itself. That unity is Christ.

A further question nags the critical lay mind. Who collected these writings and for what purpose? Is the Bible planned propaganda? The historical evidence is incontrovertible; the collection was not planned by the men who wrote the documents. Those first generation Christians did not set out to produce the New Testament. They wrote as the prophets had spoken— for God to persons *in* historical situations. But there was a new dimension: the long-awaited liberation was now a reality in Christ. This apostolic witness to God's action was recorded and collected for a practical reason; it became necessary to preserve the kerygma. When Paul wrote letters (tracts) to various Christian congregations, he put into permanent form the substance of what he had preached and taught. Luke wrote to persuade *one* man and said so. John was equally frank: "These are written that you may believe that Jesus is the Christ, the Son of God, and that believing you may have life in his name" (John 20:31). The texts vary sharply, but higher criticism has made it clear that the substance of the New Testament is in accord and unbroken continuity with what the apostles preached and taught. The New Testament writings, like the first oral proclamations, testify to the birth, life, teaching, deeds, suffering, death, resurrection, and presence of Christ. "What we preach," says Paul, "is Jesus Christ" (II Cor. 4:5). That is what the apostles preached and taught. That is what the New Testament records. That is what the Old Testament points to. That is what the church is called to proclaim—Jesus as the Christ, crucified, resurrected, at work in the world.

The authority of the Bible, therefore, does not reside in an infallible text nor in ecclesiastical pronouncements; it resides in the person, work, and message of Jesus Christ. Protestants accept the Scriptures' authority because of the witness which the documents themselves bear to God's mighty deeds accomplished to win salvation for his estranged creation, man. The Bible has authority for man because it gives him Christ. Consequently, responsible Protestants judge the institutional church, its traditional forms and doctrines, and the faith and life of its members in the light of the Scriptures' witness to Christ. Luther argued that the church cannot give more force or authority to a book than the book has in itself, and that a council cannot make that to be scripture which in its own nature is not scripture. His argument is as telling today as it was in the sixteenth century. So the Protestant principle holds that the Bible is the *chief authority* in the church. It also supports the claim of an open Bible because that allows God to speak *now* to the human condition.

The institutional church can *exist* by human wit. The people of God cannot *live* apart from the Word. God and man belong in the same community—if community is to exist. That is the Scriptures' witness. Bible study and theological inquiry and dialogue are essential if the church is to preach Christ. The Word in preaching and sacraments was committed to the church by God. Therefore, any plan, program, decision, or act which is not in accord with his Word is "unconstitutional" in his sight! Membership policies, benevolence objectives, church school curricula, the work of evangelism, candidates for the official board, interchurch cooperation, building programs, staff salaries, political philosophies—everything—must be examined, discussed, and decided in the light of God's Word. The faith and life of the church and its institutional forms must be brought under the lordship of Christ, even as the Scriptures' witness (prophets and apostles) must also be interpreted in the light of his person and teaching. This is the church's primary authority.

The Scriptures are like the flesh and blood in which Christ came into history as a man. The Bible provides the inspired record of God's self-revelation inside human experience. If "there had been no such written record, there would be no such thing in the world today as faith in God through Jesus Christ, and the life of Jesus would be a forgotten episode in the world's history." [18]

Nygren provides a concise summary.

*Revelation* is the activity of God, his active and effective intervention in human life. It reaches its height in God's action in Christ. The Bible is the message about this action; but *this message is itself an action of God.* When it is proclaimed, the fact is that God continues and completes his action in us. When the gospel is preached, God releases men from the dominion of the powers of destruction and makes them members of a new humanity whose Lord and head is Christ.[19]

[18] Charles M. Jacobs, *What Then Is Christianity?* Philadelphia: Fortress Press, 1940), p. 132.
[19] *The Significance of the Bible for the Church*, p. 36.

## Questions for Discussion

1. Freedom without discipline ends in anarchy; and discipline without freedom ends in tyranny. Discuss this historically and apply it to the parish.
2. What do you understand by the phrase *sola scriptura*?
3. Since the Reformation church recovered and exalted *sola scriptura,* how have diversity, exclusiveness, and acrimony gotten into the marrow of Protestantism? How does this affect the church in your community?
4. What are the chief characteristics of the fundamentalist view of Scripture? Of the existentialist view (Bultmann, Tillich, Bonhoeffer)?
5. What is the difference between myth and fairy tale? Between myth and legend?
6. I described the American parish as "the last refuge of unbridled individualism." Do you agree?
7. Is there a "historical Jesus"? On what evidence do you base your view?
8. Does your parish accept Christ as the Lord of Scripture? Do you? How then is Scripture to be interpreted?

# 3

# The Biblical Shape
# of the Church

*On this rock I will build my church.*

*The Church's one foundation*
*Is Jesus Christ her Lord.*

—SAMUEL JOHN STONE

The Word of God comes to full expression in
Jesus Christ. The inspired human record of God's
self-revelation is the Bible. The Scriptures testify to
Christ's person, work, and message which constitute
the evangel (good news). The church, biblically
viewed, is the extension in time of the Resurrection
Christ through historical forms. It is the body of the
living Christ. Entrusted by God to his church, Christ
gets into the world through persons committed to
him.

The church is not an accidental, secondary element in
in the Christian faith—as if God had really willed to
save individuals, who through misguided gregarious in-
stinct and evil power-impulses mistakenly formed for
themselves a community of worship. Rather . . . the
church . . . is a fundamental part of the divine purpose,
willed by God and established by him just as much as
the Incarnation itself. . . . The church, therefore, is a
vital part of the gospel itself.[1]

[1] Langdon Gilkey, *How the Church Can Minister to the
World Without Losing Itself* (New York: Harper & Row,
1964), pp. 60-61.

The church is not a human invention. God created it through persons responsive to him; its life is his Word. On *that* the Reformers agreed. So did the early church. Its first creedal statement, after affirming the triune God, speaks straightway about the church which he fashions: "I believe in the Holy Spirit, the holy catholic Church, the communion of saints." [2] The church is God's idea and handiwork; he employs it to carry on his Son's ministry to save the world. That is the Scriptures' witness. History confirms it. Unfortunately, many contemporary laymen do not think and speak of the church in that fashion.

The denominational churchman, asked about the church to which he belongs, replies that "his" church is large or small; modernistic, colonial, or Gothic; liturgical or nonliturgical; urban, suburban, or rural; involved in the life of the community or isolated. He may talk about the youth program, the educational opportunities, and the preaching in his church. He may also quote a line or two from Berger, Cox, or Robinson. But the Bible, Christ, and personal commitment are not considered seriously at any of these levels of discussion—institutional, functional, sociological.

The sectarian Christian on the other hand discusses the Bible, Christ, and personal commitment but says little about the church. His testimony is individualistic and personalistic. He presents the Bible as a collection of doctrines to be accepted or as a set of rules to be followed. He judges personal commitment

---

[2] The Apostles' Creed, the oldest and most widely used of the statements of Christian faith, has had no subtractions in eighteen centuries and no additions in thirteen centuries.

on grounds of "right" belief and moralistic behavior. His human piety muffles the voice of the living God. The sectarian Christian acknowledges God, speaks openly about him, yet disavows his will and presumes on his love.

Of course, these sketches of the Protestant laity are deliberately overdrawn. Actually, there is a growing core of laymen in church and sect—concerned, educated, searching—who exhibit firm biblical insights and whose loyalty to Christ is existential. They are the church's hope. But they are a remnant. Most Protestant laymen in this generation do not orient to a *biblical* image of the church or demonstrate a viable way of witnessing.

This lack, however, is not new in American church life. Sixty years ago, Charles E. Jefferson, delivering the Beecher Lectures at Yale, observed that "the church has, to many Christians, become an object to be apologized for, and has ceased to be an institution to be sacrificed for and loved." [3] Parish leaders who seriously want renewal will learn first to discern the Scriptures' witness to the living Word and accept its authority. They will go before the tribunal of biblical evidence to discern the biblical shape of the church. Parish renewal requires that clerical and lay leaders compare their personal, denominational, and cultural images of the church with the biblical image. The Bible provides the objective frame of reference for making sound, practical changes in their thinking and decision-making.

Viewed sweepingly, the Scriptures describe the

[3] Jefferson, *The Building of the Church* (New York: The Macmillan Company, 1910), p. 9.

church as people attracted to Christ, committed to his person, convinced of his presence, living in fellowship with him and through him with one another, allowing him to use them as cross-bearers to persuade the world that he is Lord and Savior—all this in response to God's deed in Christ. That is the biblical picture of Jesus and his disciples. Essentially, it is the biblical shape of the church as it comes into clearer view in the Book of Acts and in Paul's letters. The Word in preaching-teaching and sacraments and people hearing and doing that truth constitute the church. The church is Christ and people bound inextricably into community.

Scripture admits readily to the human disabilities of the Christ-believers. It reports that Judas, part of the nucleus of the new community, defected and that every apostle faltered badly. The New Testament does not hide the dark stains and gray patches on the fabric of life in the early Christian community: Ananias and Sapphira cheated; Demas quit; Peter denied his Lord; John Mark ran home for a season; the Corinthians were stingy; the Galatians were taken in by false teachers. And Paul—often impatient, occasionally angry—called a time or two for excluding church members on the grounds of pagan behavior. Fortunately, the maturing church honored Jesus' criterion for judgment: "Let both [the wheat and tares] grow together until the harvest" (Matt. 13:24-30, 36-43).

To call the church "holy," therefore, is to have one's eye fixed on Christ and his gospel, not on man and his performance. The church is holy (acceptable to God) when the Word is proclaimed and taught, heard and heeded. It is a unique gathering of God's people insofar as the members accept Christ's authority, claim his promises, and do his commandments. The Word and man can get together! Scripture shows that the Macedonian church gave beyond its means; the Philippians' support of Paul kept him from growing weary in well-doing; Luke reclaimed John Mark for the ministry; the hard-pressed congregations in Asia Minor provided money for their beleaguered co-workers in Jerusalem. The people of God are unique in the quality of their concern and their style of life when they hear and heed his Word.

Scripture is also firm on the particularity of the church. The old covenant was established by God with a particular people, the Israelites. The new covenant fulfilled that specific relationship. Jesus' choice of twelve disciples (twelve tribes of Israel) demonstrated to the Jewish people the vital link between the old and the new. The apostolic church remembered and proclaimed an event in human history, not a philosophical concept or a system of ethics. It shared this good news with the Jews first and then with the Gentiles. Paul addressed the believers in particular places—Corinth, Rome, Ephesus. The church is particularistic because God acted and continues to act in human history. Jesus was born to a Jewish woman during the reign of Caesar Augustus. He suffered, was crucified, died, and was raised from the dead during the governorship of Pontius Pilate. In the Resurrection Christ, God continues to act in history. The church exists to proclaim that man's liberation from sin, death, and guilt is accomplished by God in Christ.

Christianity, as William Temple insisted vigorously, is the most materialistic among the world's religions. It lives on the event of God-in-Christ proclaimed, heard, and accepted by particluar people in particular places at particular times through specific acts of worship, witness, and service. The layman's intuitive awareness that he *can* cherish a local loyalty is biblical. The psalmist—"let us go to the house of the Lord"—meant the temple in Jerusalem. Jesus attended a particular synagogue; he worshiped in *the* temple at Jerusalem. The layman's loyalty to a particular congregation is wholesome so long as he recognizes that God is not confined to that congregation or possessed by its denomination. Baptists and Episcopalians, Mennonites and Roman Catholics—all Christians—must keep "their" doctrine of the church worthy of the largeness of the gospel of God. The early church underscored both particularity and universality when it described itself as the "communion of saints."

This biblical view suggests criteria for parish leaders seeking renewal in the congregation where their judgments are decisive. Does our congregation curtail the largeness of the gospel by practicing an exclusive membership policy? "We are born Lutheran." Do we actively seek Negroes, social aristocrats, intellectuals, the poverty ridden, teen-age rebels, the unchurched as members? "They wouldn't be at home here." Does our congregation wink at biblical doctrine by adhering to a membership policy which neglects to instruct youth and adults in the faith? "It's not what we believe, but what we do that matters." Do we cajole people into "joining" our association of like-minded people? "We need you. You will help us!" Is our congregation involved in Christ's mission to all people? "Build the plant; benevolence be hanged." Is our denomination seeking ecumenical relationships at the expense of loyalty to the Christ of the Scriptures? "Let's get together now and settle our differences later." Is our denomination resisting unity in Christ by revering its cherished traditions—dogma, liturgy, polity? "They are not confessional, liturgical, episcopal." The clergy do not have, and in most cases do not want, a monopoly in deciding these questions. The laity must decide them before the tribunal of biblical evidence.

In the light of these introductory observations I shall outline three practical approaches for understanding the church in the light of Scripture. The first employs figurative language (images). The second uses nonfigurative language (ideas and concepts). The third employs both approaches. None is a panacea, but each will open some minds and hearts to the Holy Spirit.

## I

One approach—the use of images—exposes laymen to an unfamiliar way of conscious thinking. Most Americans "think" empirically. But they react and respond to images more than they realize. An image, Webster states, is "a mental representation of anything not actually present to the senses." Uncle Sam —bewhiskered, kind of countenance, dressed in red-and-white-striped pants and blue coat—is an image of the United States. The National League football team at Baltimore is called the Colts. Neither description is to be taken literally. The United States has different faces and innumerable layers of reality which "Uncle Sam" does not convey. The Baltimore football players do not have four legs apiece. Images are *pictures* in the mind. The New Testament is crammed with "pictures" of the church which were employed usefully when the church was young. Examined and understood in historical context, these images can be enlightening for many twentieth-century churchmen.

Paul Minear, reporting on the research of scholars commissioned to study the church in the New Testament, identifies some thirty images which the apostolic writers employed—among them the body of Christ, the bride of Christ, the new community. He classifies these images into three groups, each indicative of the context within which the Christian community itself was viewed. First, there are those images which gravitate around the conception of the church as the *people of God*. The second group of images gravitates around the activity of God in creating a *new humanity* (cosmic beginning, location, destiny). Third, there are images which gravitate around the conception of the church as a *fellowship of saints* (believers) whose life together demonstrates its unique quality.[4]

To wrestle with these New Testament images of the church in a yearlong study will enrich Christian lives and sharpen the church's witness. Clergymen, if only to review their seminary course in the New Testament, will profit from this study. Laymen will

[4] Minear, *Images of the Church in the New Testament* (New York: Harper & Row, 1960).

have their cultural images of the church shattered and relevant images defined. This course of study is exacting. The teacher must be an informed churchman as well as a competent student of the Bible. Carefully prepared for each session, he will emphasize that each image (figurative language) makes one major point—namely, unity: the body of *Christ*, the people of *God*, the fellowship of *believers*.[5] He will underscore the Scriptures' witness: every image presents the church as being inseparable from the gospel, inextricably bound up in God's action.

The key figures of the Reformation, captivated and enlightened by the biblical shape of the church, defined the ecclesia as the assembly of believers where the Word is preached and the sacraments are administered.[6] All else, they said, was adiaphorous. Their view of the church, shaped to the biblical image, was a *radical* attack on the complexly institutionalized, impersonal, bureaucratized church of the Middle Ages. Primarily, they respected only one tradition—the Scriptures.

Using Minear's book as a guide and Scripture as the resource, selected laymen can be exposed to the biblical image of the church. Each student must work diligently to "get inside" the apostolic mind, acquire some knowledge of the dominant world view of the first century, and prepare himself to accept the early church, "warts and all." The study will be profitable for some, not all. But there are other ways to get at the biblical image of the church.

---

[5] There are secondary insights provided by each image, but, like Jesus' parables, each image carries a single thrust.

[6] John Calvin added a third mark of the church—discipline.

## II

Another approach to understanding the biblical shape of the church depends on nonfigurative language—concepts and descriptions. It calls for the student to dig into Luke, Acts, John, and the Pauline epistles with these questions before him: Where does the "new community" first appear? How does it develop? What is its nature and purpose? He discovers quickly that the new community took shape at the inception of Jesus' ministry. Jesus chose, taught, commissioned, and sent his little flock into the world to declare: "The kingdom of God is at hand; repent, and believe in the gospel."

The view that Jesus did not establish a church goes to pieces when it is hailed before the tribunal of biblical evidence. Scripture leaves no doubt that he *called* the twelve disciples, *taught* them intensively, and *sent* them into the world to carry on in his strength what he had initiated. The argument (based on Harnack's view) that the church was established by Jesus' first-century followers—who in turn corrupted the simplicity and purity of his message—is refuted by most critical studies. Contemporary biblical scholarship traces a clear line from Jesus and his disciples through the primitive church in Jerusalem to the churches of Paul and John. Summarizing the results of this scholarship, Archibald M. Hunter sets down from Scripture four arguments that Jesus deliberately fashioned a new Israel, ecclesia, the church.

(1) The Kingdom of God, which lies at the heart of Jesus' words and works, necessarily implies a New People of God.

(2) The idea of Messiahship, as Jesus interpreted it, implies the gathering of a community.

(3) The Shepherd must needs have a flock: When Jesus speaks of himself as doing a Shepherd's work and of his disciples as a flock, he is describing his Messianic task of gathering the people of God.

(4) That Jesus called twelve disciples . . . taught them . . . sent them . . . instituted a covenant with them— all these facts show Jesus deliberately executing his Messianic task of creating a new Israel, the true people of God.[7]

First, Jesus faced humanity's elemental temptations which tested *his* loyalty to God. Victorious, he proceeded to select twelve disciples after an extended season of prayer. He befriended the men he chose, lived with them, indoctrinated them, entrusted his message to them, disciplined them, and sent them out to preach and teach the good news. He viewed his school (disciples) as the refashioned community of Israel bound by a *new* covenant between God and his people, and said so plainly. The biblical record confirms that Jesus spoke more often about the kingdom of God than about the church (ecclesia). But it also testifies that he viewed his new community as the beachhead of God's kingdom, describing it as leaven, light, salt. He encouraged his little flock, promised them God's providential care, assured them of his abiding presence, and, resurrected, gave substance to that assurance. The expanding little flock— convinced that they had a message to proclaim, em-

---

[7] *The Message of the New Testament* (Philadelphia: The Westminster Press, 1944), pp. 53-62.

powered by the presence of the Resurrection Christ, filled with the Holy Spirit—exercised Christ's ministry *in the world* so effectively that they were denounced, imprisoned, beaten, stoned, exiled, crucified. The early church understood Paul when he talked about the treasure in earthen vessels, the light and the lamp, the new creature in Christ. That was *their* experience, too.

This new community of persons, accepting Jesus as Lord, embodied the person of the Resurrection Christ, taking him *and* his gospel for its message. Consequently, the Reformers, searching the Scriptures, stated simply that the church is the assembly of believers where the Word of God is preached and taught and the sacraments are administered. Through these human activities (preaching and teaching) and material means (water, bread, and wine) the living Word seeks out and confronts persons who, in their freedom, accept or reject Christ. Churchmen who stand existentially in the apostolic tradition know that salvation is in and through the church. In this context, "true Christian experience is always ecclesiastical experience." [8]

From the beginning, the Christian church fashioned evangelical forms (a) to persuade persons to embrace Christ and to care for them in its community, (b) to preserve and defend apostolic truth (kerygma), and (c) to carry the promises and demands of Christ into the world. The kerygma—oral tradition—began to take form in writing about A.D. 50. Before the end of the century, both the kerygma and didache (apos-

[8] J. S. Whale, *Christian Doctrine* (New York: The Macmillan Company, 1941), p. 19.

tolic teaching) were in written form. The New Testament canon was fixed by A.D. 400. The written tradition, creedal statements, and basic doctrines were fashioned during the first centuries to preserve the kerygma and defend it against heretical views, especially the docetic view of Christ which makes him less than human and robs him of historical relevance, and the Arian view of man which sees him as an essential contributor to his own salvation.

Christianity has been able to bridge the centuries by providing a Spirit-inhabited institution through which the Word has become flesh in each succeeding generation. The historical Jesus, a child of his times, did not envision the medieval ecclesiastical hierarchy, the Industrial Revolution, "the garbled lexicon of quantum physics," presidential elections, the cold war, or orbital flights. His church, however, has lived to see and experience all these and more. Led by his Spirit it has shaped historical forms through which he has confronted persons in time, from within which it could be and through which it could accomplish God's mission.

The sixteenth-century Reformation was, in part, a criticism of the hierarchical Christianity developed during the Middle Ages, but the Reformers could not escape institutional forms. Century by century, generation by generation, week by week, the church must bring its forms and organizational patterns under the searching judgment of the Word to discern whether they are means or ends. But the church cannot disdain institutional forms; they are necessary means. Biblically viewed, order is established and maintained for the sake of freedom. Good order, therefore, does not require uniformity. It exists wherever any witness to the gospel persuades persons to decide *for* or *against* Christ. That is the only valid test for dogma, creed, liturgy, polity, or program: a decision for or against Christ.

Neither Scripture nor Christian history provides solid ground for arguing that any one pattern of organization or any single form of worship prevailed in the early church. There were varieties of Christian experience; the Bible bristles with them. There were varieties of liturgical forms; Christian history is crammed with them. No single liturgy is suitable to every man's worship experience. Man's response to the Word in preaching and teaching and the sacraments *is* Christian worship. A liturgy which is relevant today—simple or rich, traditional or newly fashioned—may be archaic next year. Forms which were meaningful in the sixteenth century can be excitingly relevant for some Christians today. The issue is not either-or; it is both-and. Multiple worship services *and* varied liturgical forms will be offered by the parish that wants to help contemporary man to worship God. The responsible parish will also provide learning opportunities for men and women and children at times and on days other than the fixed Sunday school hour. It will provide opportunities for dialogue which an effective preaching-teaching ministry always creates. However varied, new or old, those forms and patterns which allow the Holy Spirit to move freely are means, not ends.

A study of the new community as it emerges in Luke, Acts, John, and the Pauline epistles demonstrates that the church exercised Christ's preaching-teaching-healing ministry. Consequently, parish leaders who orient to the biblical image will administer the congregation where they worship, learn, and serve so that it (a) proclaims and teaches the Word of God relevantly, (b) preserves and defends apostolic truth (kerygma and didache) flexibly but firmly, and (c) motivates and equips its members to render priestly service to persons and to witness persuasively in the world.

*Preaching and Teaching.* Scripture testifies that the primary objective of all Christian ministry is to bring salvation to the human spirit. This divine objective calls for the bold proclamation of the good news that God acted decisively in Jesus to liberate man from sin, demoniac forces, and death; and that the church provides the means to meet this saving God in Word and sacrament. At the outset of his ministry, Jesus entered the local synagogue, read from Isaiah, laid the scroll aside, and declared the fulfillment of prophecy: "He has sent me to proclaim release to the captives." Christ came to break man's bondage to sin, death, and the devil. He established and commissioned his community (ecclesia) to share him and his message, assuring them that those whose sins they forgave in his Name, God would forgive.

The church exists to preach and teach Christ. From the beginning, it has remembered—albeit unevenly —that Jesus came preaching (Luke 4:42-44). The apostles ceased not to preach and teach Christ daily (Acts 2:10). Following Pentecost, the church took to proclaiming that "Jesus is Lord" and teaching Christianity as "the Way" in its growing assemblies, in the intimacy of its constituent homes, in the dialogues of friendship, and in the give-and-take of the shops and the marketplaces. Proclamation was to one person, several, *and* many. The current notion that preaching is ineffectual because—so the argument goes—the gospel can be communicated only in small groups is at odds with the biblical image of the church's ministry. Peter's preaching claimed five thousand converts at a single service (Acts 4:4). The early church—unacquainted with group dynamics, role playing, and dialogue—would have applauded Kierkegaarde: "The Word divides a crowd into individuals." The Word in preaching does reach out, lay hold on, and motivate persons, even as those persons are in the midst of a crowd. The ordained minister preaches. But that ministry is a function of the whole church; every Christian is called to exercise it and participate in it.

Forthright biblical preaching which avoids the marginal (shallow moralism), penetrates to the heart of man's profound dilemma (meaninglessness and guilt), and speaks to his desperate loneliness (fragmented person), persuades some persons to repent, encourages them to trust God, and restores them to their true identity. Linked with evangelical teaching, it motivates and equips them to exercise Christ's ministry in the world. Apart from biblical preaching, worship becomes esoteric or perfunctory; the sacraments are viewed as cultic rights or mechanical tests for membership; evangelism remains a human activity; stewardship is equated with raising the budget.

Primary functions of the church's ministry are biblical preaching and evangelical teaching. That is how men, in their freedom, are persuaded to follow Christ and enabled and equipped to understand his message and to witness intelligibly in the world. The church exists to persuade, nurture, equip, and refurbish men in the Faith. That purpose calls for proclamation and teaching—functions of ministry which the church was fashioned to exercise. "The necessity of preaching resides in the fact that when God saves a man through Christ he insists on a living, personal encounter with him here and now in the sphere of present personal relationships." [9] That responsibility rests squarely on the priesthood of believers.

*Guarding Apostolic Truth.* It is the historic task of the church not only to proclaim and teach apostolic truth but to be its *custodian.* Friedrich Gogarten warns that the two most serious threats to the gospel against which it must be protected today are its being dissolved into a myth and its being hardened into a religion of law.[10] We examined those dangers in Chapter 2 and concluded that the absolute demythologizer and the hardened fundamentalist must be resisted and confronted. The church must protect the gospel from being dissolved into a myth or hardened into a religion of law.

But there are other serious threats to the gospel in the twentieth century, especially in America. A new American religion, "Protestant-Catholic-Jew," blurs the particularist genius of each and argues beguilingly that "We're all headed for the same place." [11] There is a "new paganism" which values human experience

---

[9] H. H. Farmer, *The Servant of the Word* (New York: Charles Scribner's Sons, 1942), p. 27.

[10] Quoted in *Christianity and Crisis,* April 27, 1964.

[11] Will Herberg, *Protestant—Catholic—Jew* (Garden City: Doubleday, 1955).

primarily in terms of the five senses. There is the lack-luster parish which presents the gospel in forms and styles which make it appear to be irrelevant. Equally dangerous is the "gung-ho" parish which is so eager to be relevant that it obscures or ignores the fundamentals of the Faith. Succeeding chapters underscore the biblical strategy and suggest tactics for defending and preserving the gospel—one of the central tasks of the church. This requires consecrated scholars, a relevant theology, and persuasive preachers—ordained and lay.

*Doing the Truth.* The church exists to do Christ's commandments. It is fashioned to act out the Truth in the world. This calls for priestly service to all sorts of people without regard for their condition, color, or creed. It also requires a person-to-person witness which is intelligible to secular man in *his* cultural setting. It requires equally that each congregation bring persons, ideas, mores, and institutions under the judgment of God's Word. All three responsibilities, accepted by persons in concrete situations, produce tension and incite conflict.

But getting the gospel into the world requires not only a disciplined personnel; it also requires money. Church members generally refer to this aspect of churchmanship as "benevolence giving." Whether the congregation employs a unified budget, pledge cards, and envelopes, or relies on love gifts, the issue is the same: until the local congregation uses "unrighteous mammon" to make friends for the kingdom, it is the maimed body of Christ. Scripture testifies that the church, from the beginning, was concerned to provide material gifts for widows and orphans and Gentiles beyond its own boundaries. To bicker and argue over benevolence, to drag one's feet, as some official boards and congregations do, fractures the biblical image of the church. That needs to be said plainly in parish after parish.

But benevolence is not simply outreach through the church-at-large. It is "inreach" too. Responsible parish leaders will define and administer a benevolence program which provides groceries for hard-pressed parishioners, the cost of psychiatric help for those who cannot afford it, scholarship aid for promising youth who are living in economically hard-pressed homes. The congregation will also provide blood donors, regular lay visitors among the elderly and shut-ins, and laymen from business, the professions, and the trades to provide vocational counseling for the parish youth and their friends. "Living together in Christ" produces a community in which clergy counsel parishioners, laymen counsel clergy, mates counsel each other, parents counsel children, and youth counsel parents—from the resources of the Word. Truth is spoken in love by persons to persons in the renewed parish so that each can realize his true humanity in Christ.[12]

If a congregation is not open to all races and to all conditions of people—prodigals and prostitutes, rebels and discreet sinners; if persons in marital trouble and teen-agers with personal problems do not come confidently to the clergy and lay teachers in the congregation—as the prodigal son arose and came to his father—that congregation is not reflecting the biblical

[12] See *From Tradition to Mission*, chap. 6, "Living Together at Trinity."

image of the church. The church exists to do Christ's commandments, to live the Truth, to be Christ-bearers in the world.

## III

A third approach to understanding what the church is calls for a study of the Gospels and Pauline epistles with one eye on Christology and the other on ecclesiology. Paul had two main themes in his preaching —Christ and the church. That is the structure of this particular teaching thrust. The church exists wherever its members remember (a) that they have a given place in a unique fellowship, a redeemed fellowship, bought for a price—the life of its Lord and Savior Jesus Christ; and (b) that this unique fellowship in which they live was purchased to do God's work in the world.

The first strand in this biblical description is the kerygma, the good news, the message of salvation, the proclamation of Christ's sacrificial life, death, and resurrection. This event and message call for declaration and demonstration, not argumentation. This message and deed were given by God to persuade persons to accept Christ. Luther was historical and existential when he declared: "I believe that Jesus Christ . . . has redeemed me, a lost and condemned creature, . . . not with gold or silver, but with His holy, precious blood . . . that I may be His own and live under Him in His kingdom, and serve Him in everlasting righteousness, innocence, and blessedness." [13]

---

[13] Luther's explanation of the second article of the Apostles' Creed in *The Small Catechism*.

The objective and subjective characteristics of faith are stressed equally.

Divine deed and human response, God's grace and man's faith, Christ and his people make the church. The church exists where the Word is preached (taught) and the sacraments administered among persons who, persuaded to look upon the empty Cross, declare, "There was no other way; Christ died for me," nurture their new life from the gospel, and go out to share it with others.

Obviously, there are dangers in this elemental approach. They were there in the beginning. Paul warned against them. Mature churchmen in this generation are alert to them, too. An uncritical reliance on the sacrificial Rescuer can calcify into rigid dogma; fundamentalists err here. An undiscerning dependence on the Cross of Christ can be fashioned into a verbal shibboleth; all Protestant and Roman Catholic churchmen must guard against this error. A thoughtless faith in a self-giving Savior can deteriorate into maudlin sentimentality; the contemporary parish has been castigated for this. A carefully hedged commitment to Christ can end in dependence on "cheap grace"; Bonhoeffer alerted all Christians to this danger.

But the caricature of truth does not alter its reality. History testifies that Christ atoned for man's sin on Calvary. His deed fashioned a new situation for every man—each in his freedom *can* go home again. That is the objective aspect of Christ's death and resurrection. But each man must decide to arise and go to his father. Repentance and obedience comprise the subjective aspect. Both aspects are necessary for man's

salvation. Wherever a few or many accept, believe in,
confess, and share Christ's hard-won victory over sin,
death, and the devil, the church comes into being,
matures, and moves into the world with banners flying. It is this community which ushers in a corner of
God's kingdom.[14] The church exists wherever persons accept and confess that they are bought, called,
gathered, and preserved in the Faith. The church does
not exist simply because individual congregations in
association with other congregations "possess" the gospel; the gospel must also possess men and women and
boys and girls in those congregations. Otherwise,
there is no church. Luther put it concisely:

Wherever, therefore, you hear or see this Word preached,
believed, confessed, and acted on, there do not doubt
that there must be a true ecclesia sancta catholica, a
Christian, holy people, even though it be small in num-
bers; for God's Word does not go away empty (Isaiah
1v), but must have at least a fourth part, or a piece of the
field. If there were no other mark than this one alone,
it would still be enough to show that there must be a
Christian church there; for God's Word cannot be present
without God's people, and God's people cannot be without God's Word.[15]

The living church remembers that it was bought
at a price. It remembers equally that it was purchased
for a purpose: to worship the Father of its Lord Jesus
Christ and to witness to his lordship in the world. In

[14] James Stewart, *A Faith to Proclaim* (New York and Nashville: Abingdon-Cokesbury, 1946), treats this magnificently.
Many laymen will find him readable.

[15] "On the Councils and the Churches," *Works of Martin
Luther* (Philadelphia: Muhlenberg Press, 1931), V, 271.

biblical perspective, worship and witness are inseparable. Presently, however, there are churchmen who
call for witness without regard for worship and others
who become so preoccupied with worship forms that
they show little concern for an active witness in the
world. Parish leaders, orienting to the biblical image
of the church, guard against both errors. If worship
does not constrain one to witness in the world, it is
pretense: "Why do you call me 'Lord, Lord,' and not
do what I tell you?" (Luke 6:46). Biblically viewed,
witness is the continuing act of Christian worship.
Essentially, worship *is* Christian witness. Churchmen
committed to Christ do not treat worship as an elec-
tive nor denigrate the preaching and teaching of the
Word.

In the hour of Christian worship the drama of
salvation is reenacted, the event of God in Christ is
focused on the screen of contemporary life, the holy
God confronts man in his sin and, baring a father's
heart, bids him come home. The living Word—
Christ himself—comes to worshiping man in the human words and activities of preaching and teaching
and in the earthly materials of the sacraments. Some
worshipers are indifferent. Others are offended. But
some, moved to accept Christ as Lord and Savior,
nurture that relationship from the Word. Those who
acknowledge their need and accept God's redemptive
act respond with confession, hymns of praise, and the
giving of themselves to Christ. They go out to sin
again and know it. They also go out to witness—one
to face a beguiling temptation with new insights; another to stand alone in some significant controversy
because his conscience is captive to the Word; and

still another to cope heroically with the newfound knowledge of a killing disease. The "new community" is at work in the world. The redeemed community, gathered to worship and learn, is motivated by the Holy Spirit to witness in the world—the *only* arena there is.[16]

Actually, those who worship the God of the prophets, the Father of Christ, are more daring than others. "The worship of God," Whitehead observes, "is not a rule of safety." Indeed, Christian worshipers are more worldly than other people. That is history's testimony. Wesley and his lay preachers went into the dirtiest corners of poverty-ridden London in mid-eighteenth century. Kagawa rendered priestly service in the slums of Yokohama. Bishop Dibelius, speaking against the Nazis in the early 1930's, was denied his pulpit by the Fuehrer before World War II. Bonhoeffer was hanged for his active part in the abortive bomb plot against Hitler in 1944. Authentic Christians are indeed more worldly than "company men," union leaders, military heroes, beatniks, and the readers of *Playboy* magazine. One remembers especially how— in those first costly centuries of the church—slaves, merchants, fishermen, and Roman soldiers worshiped God in private homes and catacombs and got so involved *in the world* that, centuries later, the historian Edward Gibbon, surprised and angered at their influence, charged them with the fall of the Roman Empire! The church moves into the world with banners flying when it remembers that it was bought for a price and for a purpose.

[16] For a fuller description of worship in the parish church, see *From Tradition to Mission*, pp. 139-43.

We have suggested three biblical approaches to understanding the nature and purpose of the church. There is no magic in any of them, but there is truth in all three. To get at that truth requires competent leadership and critical cooperation.

## Questions for Discussion

1. How do you describe your church when you speak of it to others? Be candid.
2. What do you understand by the terms "biblical preaching," "evangelical teaching," "shepherding," "church administration," "ecumenicity," and "social action"?
3. Identify and discuss the characteristics of the biblical image of the church. Apply these to your parish as measure and guide.
4. Do you believe that *your* congregation embodies Christ? How do you demonstrate *your* belief?
5. In what sense is the church universal? particularistic? holy?
6. Does your congregation share eagerly in the life and witness of the church? What is its attitude toward and relationship with its denomination, local council of churches, National Council of Churches, and World Council of Churches?
7. "We're all headed for the same place and there is so much evil to overcome that we can't be bothered over theological differences." Discuss.
8. Is Christ the Lord of "your church"? Is he Lord in your life? Strive for honest dialogue.

# 4

# The Significance
# of Leadership

*Before the gates of excellence the high gods
have placed sweat.*
—HESIOD

*We have each to determine whether this
world is an arena where we fight to get
what we can for ourselves, or a field of
honor where we give all we can for our
fellowmen.*
—WILFRED T. GRENFELL

---

Leadership in the church resides in the communion
of believers. The exercise of Christ's ministry is corporate. The power of the witness inherent in that
corporate ministry is dependent on the Holy Spirit.
The effective deployment of that power requires order, and order requires organization and leadership.
If, as Halford Luccock once observed, a sermon can
splatter gelatinously around the walls of the sanctuary
for want of a skeletal outline, so too can a parish,
lacking sound institutional forms and competent
leadership, dissipate the Spirit's work.

The church, from the beginning, created forms and
produced leaders. The disciples elected Matthias to
the seat vacated by Judas and appointed fellow believers to wait on tables so that they could preach and
teach Christ without interruption. Peter, Paul, Luke,
and others trained pastoral leaders. Paul's counsel to
Timothy on the qualifications of a congregational
overseer (bishop) is practical today. The Apostle's

confrontation of Peter at Jerusalem was a sharp demonstration of constructive leadership. The early church produced leaders and fashioned forms so that Christ's ministry—the church's primary function—could be exercised effectively.

But the pristine Christian community did not establish an order for its pastoral leaders or define set forms. It viewed ministry as a function to be exercised by every member in the fellowship of believers according to his consecration and competence. The ministry of the Word is a function, a task to be performed. It is not an order. As a means of grace it belongs to the people of God, the community of believers, the church. Each believer is under constraint to bear witness to his faith in God's Word. This is the priesthood of believers. But this community needs consecrated leadership. Luther defined that clearly: "We are all priests, but we are not all clergymen." Recently, Karl Barth's longtime colleague, Eduard Thurneysen, a parish pastor, put the need bluntly: "It is the minister before others who has the credentials for pastoral care in that he is ordained and chosen as the shepherd of the congregation." [1]

The responsibility for exercising Christ's ministry centers in the ordained clergy, but it does not end there. It is the joint responsibility of the clergy and the laity, the people of God. It is a perversion of the concept of the priesthood of believers to allow Christ's ministry to rest solely on the ordained minister(s) and a few parish leaders. But it is an equally unrealistic reading of the concept to assume that the laity are

[1] *A Theology of Pastoral Care* (Richmond: John Knox Press, 1962), p. 235.

waiting eagerly in the wings to witness and render priestly service.[2] The people of God must be motivated and equipped to exercise it.

This situation, however, is not new. The apostolic leaders faced it boldly. Paul addressed it steadily. Generation after generation the laity have been persuaded, motivated, enlightened, equipped, and supported from the resources of God's Word (I Peter 5: 1-4). They have always needed a script, a producer, a prompter, a lead actor. That is a basic reason for choosing and ordaining pastors, one purpose of a full-time trained ministry, called and approved by the church. Pastoral leadership is integral to parish renewal. Shepherding is preeminently, but not exclusively, the ordained minister's responsibility.

The disposition of some churchmen to expect the laity to rise and reform the church because they suggest it, is naïve. Renewal does not come by clerical exhortation or ecclesiastical directive. One may as well ask a regiment to take a difficult objective without a participating officer leadership. It is equally naïve to assume, as some laymen do, that it is the clergy's responsibility to revitalize the congregation without help. Competent officers without regiments do not win battles. Clergy shape and lead parishes. Congregations also shape their clergy. Paul was the same man who wrote scathingly to the church at Corinth and almost nostalgically to the church at Philippi. Jesus comforted his disciples: "Fear not, little flock, for it is your Father's good pleasure to give you the kingdom." He also castigated the scribes and Phari-

---

[2] Hendrik Kraemer, *A Theology of the Laity* (Philadelphia: The Westminster Press, 1958), p. 95.

sees, "Woe unto you, hypocrites," and drove the money-changers from the temple. Taking a leaf from Paul's imaginative description of the church, Charles Jefferson offered this counsel to divinity students at Yale in 1910.

No preacher lives to himself or dies to himself. He is an organ functioning in an organism, finding his life in the vital relations by which he is bound to other lives. His endowments and attainments are only one factor . . . , another factor of no less importance being the attainments and endowments of the Christian society. . . . He is nourished by his environment—the family of Christ. . . . He cannot grow in isolation. . . . The church cannot wisely be ignored in any comprehensive study of the preacher's work, nor can it be shoved into the background without loss.[3]

This complex interrelatedness between leader and led is a strand in secular history. The divided Union needed Abraham Lincoln desperately, but Mr. Lincoln's potential was realized during his and the nation's "ordeal by fire." Lincoln, jesting with Herndon in Illinois, would not have written his immortal second inaugural address. Britain's "finest hour" was also Winston Spencer Churchill's finest hour. The effective leader provides direction and purpose. He facilitates movement and fosters growth. But the degree to which this happens depends in part on the capacity and openness of individuals in the group and their relationships with one another. A competent leader gets more work from a group than does an inept leader, but the ablest leader gets slim results from

[3] *The Building of the Church,* pp. 4-5.

a persistently recalcitrant group. Jesus advised his disciples to depart from any community which did not respond to the good news (Matt. 10:14). His undershepherds often lack that brand of realism and flexibility.

Other factors also bear significantly on pastoral leadership: the geographic situation of the parish, its numerical strength, its ingrained temper of mind, its cultural resources, the number of churches in the community. Sociological studies are helpful in any parish situation; they are essential for renewal in many situations.[4] Critical study, careful evaluation, sound diagnosis, and a responsible deployment of personnel are prerequisites for renewal. It is sinful to waste precious ministerial resources in parishes which should be closed or merged. It is wicked to embitter a clergyman and frustrate the laity by keeping them together when in tandem they are not useful to God. Bishops, parish pastors, and lay leaders must speak more candidly on the mating of pastors and parishes—and even consider divorce in some instances—if the dignity of persons is to be preserved and the renewal of the church is to go forward. Christian compassion does not wink at reality. God is not satisfied with haphazard methods.

At the same time, ecclesiastical officials have a moral obligation to parish pastors who get into trouble with parish and community leaders because, as clergy, they decline to trim the Word of God to suit local mores or refuse to accommodate the gospel's claims

---

[4] See *From Tradition to Mission,* chap. 1, for a sociological and theological appraisal of a particular parish; and chaps. 2–5 for the practical use of that appraisal in parish renewal.

to local power structures. The clergy are called to be shepherds, "but being a shepherd isn't the same as being a sheep dog!" [5] No clergyman serves persons responsibly unless he gives his first loyalty to God. "It is not by the minister's word that the issues are decided; but it may be by his faithfulness to his Master's Word." [6] That is the core of *pastoral leadership*.

Effective leadership in the church is not a mystery; it is open to analytical appraisal. It requires a measure of courage, a dash of imagination, average intelligence, firm character, emotional resilience, balanced judgment, and hard work—as it does in any other field of human endeavor. But there is one radical difference. Pastoral leadership orients to the biblical image of ministry. Separated from that image, strong parish leaders become managers, directors, "big operators." [7] Lacking the biblical image, indecisive parish leaders become custodians of an institution, manipulators, compromisers. The biblical image of ministry is the norm for leadership in God's church if new life is to surge through it. Examine this biblical image.

God feeds and provides for the flock of Israel, appoints men to exercise his ministry, and holds each appointee accountable for the welfare of the persons entrusted to him (2 Kings 22:16-20; Jer. 3:15, and Ezek. 34:2). God chastises careless shepherds for

[5] W. E. Sangster, *The Craft of Sermon Construction* (Philadelphia: The Westminster Press, 1951), p. 12.

[6] J. W. Stevenson, *God in My Unbelief* (New York: Harper & Row, 1963), p. 87.

[7] Niebuhr, *The Purpose of the Church and Its Ministry*, pp. 65-110.

neglecting their flocks and allowing them to be scattered (Jer. 23:1-4; 50:6). God rebukes selfish shepherds for exploiting their flocks (Ezek. 34:1-10). In the third chapter of Ezekiel, the shepherd emerges as God's bold spokesman (prophet), answerable only to God who sent him. He listens daily for God's given word to undergird, sustain, and comfort (make strong) the people committed to his care. In Isaiah (50:4-11) the prophet realizes that he strengthens the flock only insofar as he communicates God's Truth to individuals. This confrontation of persons with God's Word is his appointed task even though it brings the wrath of persons upon him. The acid test of shepherding is fidelity to the Word of the Lord.

Jesus accepted, enlarged, and fulfilled the biblical picture which emerged from Israel's custodianship of God's partial, progressive self-disclosure in the law and the prophets. When he spoke of the hireling who flees the threatened flock and identified himself as the Good Shepherd (John 10:11-16), he was not fashioning a new image; he was fulfilling and enlarging an ancient one. Demonstrating that the prophet is one who speaks for God at any cost to himself, Jesus accepted a collision course with Calvary. Obedient to the end ("My God, why . . . ?") and interceding for man ("Father, forgive them"), he gave his life ("No man takes my life") to overmatch man's rebellion against God. The church's embodiment of this suffering servant is authentic ministry. The congregation exists to expend its "given life" for the sake of the world.

This image was the picture in the minds of the apostles. Peter and John demonstrated and taught that Christ's ministers are called to please God rather than men (Acts 4:8-20). James, abhorring cheap grace, demonstrated that the good news *and* ethical instruction comprise the Word of God (James 2 and 5). Paul taught that the church exists to proclaim and teach Christ crucified, resurrected, victoriously present as the crucial event in human history. Apostolic witness is unanimous: Christians, meeting the cost of discipleship, exercise Christ's ministry. The Christian community is fashioned by the Holy Spirit to accomplish God's work in the world—the salvation of persons and the humanizing of society.

This biblical view of ministry does not focus first on the shepherd's concern for people but on his fidelity to the Word of God. Clergy and laity must come back to *that* fixed point again and again in decision after decision. The shepherd, of course, is any "new man in Christ" who, knowing that he is cared for by the Shepherd and Bishop of his soul, cares for others from Christ's own love. Christian ministry is not man-centered. It does not stem from an affable disposition, a good digestive system, or a status position in the church. Obedience to Christ—the disciplined willingness to accept his promises at face value and to wrestle with his demands—is authentic ministry. Pastoral leadership reflects Christ's authority. The shepherd cares for persons because Christ cares, motivating and equipping him to care. The authentic minister is enabled to speak God's Truth in love to persons who, like himself, are free to reject both the Truth and its bearer.

Unless the God to whom one witnesses is allowed to authenticate himself in the herald (ordained or lay), the communication of Christ is delimited sharply. Contemporary culture's preoccupation with communication—as though it were a matter of form alone rather than of content and personhood *and* form—reveals how severely "postmodern man" is alienated from God, himself, and other selves. If the parish leaders are captive to this sick culture, they obscure God's Word in the human activities of preaching, teaching, witnessing, and administering. Kierkegaard is right: where there is no God, there is no self. Both the clergy and the lay leaders must get beyond judging the ministry in terms of sincerity, personality, budgets, and attendances. Parish by parish, they must search the Scriptures to discern the biblical image of ministry and take it as the norm for ministry in their congregation. Simply defined, that ministry is biblical, whatever its form and style, which communicates God's Word to persons through persons so that each individual can decide *for* or *against* Christ. That is authentic ministry.[8]

There is overwhelming evidence that many American parishes seek to force pastors to fit cultural images of ministry rather than help them to conform to the biblical image. Father Andrew Greeley's report on the Roman Catholic Church in the suburbs addresses this reality with sympathy and perception.[9] The problems he identifies are similar to those which plague the Protestant clergy. But like the weather, this crucial problem is more talked about than attacked.

[8] *From Tradition to Mission,* chap. 2, describes in depth how one parish struggled to discern and accept the biblical image of ministry.

[9] *The Church in the Suburbs* (New York: Sheed and Ward, 1962) is good reading for parish pastors and lay leaders.

Renewal lags until clerical and lay leaders (a) discern the biblical image of ministry, (b) admit that it collides with cultural images and allow it to inform practical decisions in their parish, and (c) stand firmly against the competing cultural images which blunt authentic ministry.

No parish pastor, alone, is equal to handling this complex problem creatively. He needs the supportive insight and encouragement of concerned laymen. Paul needed Timothy and John Mark. Luther relied heavily on an able layman, Frederick, Elector of Saxony. Wesley and Whitefield would be footnotes in history except for the eager lay response to their preaching. A pastor, firm in the Faith, sound of mind, emotionally resilient, and well-grounded in biblical and theological studies, cannot exercise Christ's ministry alone. He needs colaborers, understanding, constructive criticism, and intercessory prayer.

Lay leaders must understand that their minister and his family are human beings. The clergyman is not a holy man; he is a human servant of the holy God. His family are penitent sinners, not cardboard figures of perfection. The pastor is called, if apostolic succession is taken seriously, to preach and teach God's Word, to heal persons from the resources of the Word, and to bring issues, institutions, and persons under God's judgment and grace. Whatever else the official board does, it fails God and man if it does not help its minister to be and do what God called him to be and do, joining him in that Christian vocation. That is a primary responsibility of the elected lay leaders in every congregation.

The minister, like any other Christian, must culti-

vate his commitment to Christ. Like any other citizen
he must earn a living. Like any responsible family
man, he must mature as a husband and father. Pur-
suing his vocation, he must study the Word of God
so that he understands the message he is called to
proclaim. He must also study, diagnose, and dialogue
so that he understands the American mind in general
and his community's mind in particular. These responsibilities are more than enough to consume his
time, exhaust his energies, and drain his faith. But
he must wrestle additionally with a parish and community which make demands inconsonant with his
calling. In most parishes the lay leaders, like the
membership itself, are part of the problem. They must
share in the recovery of the biblical image of ministry.
They must be among the first in the parish to re-
adjust their expectations of ministry and to evaluate
their pastor's work objectively. They must encourage
and help him and the congregation to orient to the
biblical image of ministry. The elected lay leaders
in the Protestant church bear heavy responsibility for
the exercise of Christ's ministry.

Business and professional men who expect their
pastor to be a religious organization man who manages
the church plant, oversees fund drives, and manipu-
lates persons in the interests of a businesslike institution must discard that expectation. It is not biblical.
Lay officials who view their minister as a frontier
marshal paid to keep the peace should admit that he
cannot do it without a Colt "pacifier." And that is
neither biblical nor legal! Parishioners who expect
their minister to be the Herr Pastor—a paternalist
who dispenses sage advice, visits routinely in the

hospitals, and appears with a placid "Bible sermon" each Sunday morning at eleven o'clock—need to learn the difference between a shepherd and a sheep dog.

Younger parishioners, especially in suburban churches, who view the pastor as a substitute parent for their neglected teen-agers, must admit that the New Testament provides no precedent for that expectation. These same families, convinced that the minister's *primary* responsibility is to the church school, must recognize that teaching, an elemental function of ministry, is not the only function of ministry. Parishioners who want their clergy to be officiants at communion, baptisms, weddings, and funerals must recognize that this too is only one function of ministry. Others in the parish and community who expect the clergy to be problem-solving counselors, especially for their marital hassles, must accept that pastoral counseling, a legitimate function of Christian ministry, must not crowd out the equally important functions of preaching and teaching.

Few laymen are clear on the prophetic nature of the church's ministry. Stripping away cultural images of ministry, therefore, is only a first step toward authentic witness. It is essential to drive to the heart of the *biblical* image—the shepherd-prophet—and orient to it. The shepherd cares for persons from Christ's love which requires obedience to his demands. The prophet speaks those hard demands in love. Hurt, tension, and conflict are inherent in the exercise of Christ's ministry, because segregation, war, divorce, the pill, the new morality, church and state relations are issues with which Christ's church grapples. Otherwise, it is *not* his church. This will be discussed explicitly in Chapter 5.

Recognizing and discarding false and caricatured images of ministry, taking the biblical image as a norm, the clergy and lay leaders must carry out the functions of biblical ministry—preaching, teaching, and healing. Deliberately, they must fashion an authentic ministry in the congregation in which they have been elected as overseers.

## PREACHING

Here the clergy and laity face a disconcerting situation: the world does not listen to the church. It ignores or reacts, but it does not listen. Consequently, there is little dialogue. This is due in large measure to the fact that the church itself has lost confidence in preaching. Unfortunately, too many who still expect the clergy to preach equate this function of ministry with comfortable little homilies, stylistically prefaced by a biblical text, and artfully framed to insulate the hearer against the judgment and grace of God. It is understandable that some decisive, vigorous, intelligent clergy lose heart for preaching and concentrate their energies on other functions of ministry or turn to other fields of service.

Nonetheless, Paul's question is as relevant in this century as it was in the first century: "How are they to hear without a preacher?" How indeed! Proclamation of God's liberating deed in Christ is at the center of Christianity; it always has been. A quarter of a century ago, Paul Scherer, delivering the Beecher Lectures at Yale, underscored the essential place of preaching Christ in the life of the church. "Someone has pointed out," he recalled, "that Hinduism lives by ritual and social organization, Buddhism by meditation, Confucianism by a code of manners; but Christianity lives by 'the foolishness of preaching' (I Corinthians 1:21, A. V.)." [10]

The clergy must accept that God called them to preach the gospel, to be heralds of the good news, to speak for him. Unfortunately, some ministers are part of the problem. A few, having lost confidence in the message to be proclaimed, deserve pastoral help. Others, however, have lost confidence in the human activity of preaching itself. They do not work at it— and effective preaching is *hard work*. Biblical preaching is not reserved for an intellectual elite who choose to preach as a favor to God. It is within the reach of any committed person who, possessed of emotional resilience and intellectual curiosity, accepts God's authority, honors his demands, claims his promises, and *works* at it. The living Word, personal commitment, cultural awareness, clarity, and plain speech add up to a sermon that serves God and man. The style of preaching varies from one man to another, but wherever ministers are alert, responsive, and faithful to the Word, people know from their preaching that the kingdom of God is at hand. They listen. Some come forward asking, "What must I do to become a citizen of the kingdom?" Others go away. Some, deeply hostile, reject the gospel and its bearer. All three responses demonstrate that the Word in preaching is relevant.

The laity, of course, share responsibility for effec-

[10] Scherer, *For We Have This Treasure* (New York: Harper & Bros., 1944), p. 18.

tive preaching in the parish. Their disciplined attendance at worship services, openness, and willingness to dialogue affect significantly the preacher's proclamation of the Word and their own serious response to it. God's ordained spokesmen need the insights, correction, and intelligent support of the congregation if they are to be effective preachers. Paul acknowledged that, especially to the church at Philippi. The elected lay leaders, in cooperation with clergy who work at preaching, will actively cultivate an expectant, wholesomely critical, decisive congregational mind toward preaching, because they recognize that man needs to be nurtured from the Word. It is this nurture which motivates the laity to proclaim the Word. They see preaching as a function of ministry in, for, and by the whole church.[11]

## TEACHING

Another aspect of leadership which must be strengthened centers in the teaching function of ministry. Evangelical teaching is neglected shamefully in the American parish. Most denominations, now alert to this, are providing content curricula (biblical and theological) and competent guidance. The Protestant Episcopal Church and the Lutheran Church in America produced excellent adult materials (1963-65) before they provided new and equally good content courses for children and youth. During 1967, The Methodist Church concentrated on adult educa-

---

[11] For an extended treatment on this, see *Preaching and Parish Renewal*, especially pp. 15-32. The introductions to the sermons describe the congregation's rising involvement in the preaching ministry.

tion. The United Presbyterian Church in the U.S.A., in cooperation with the United Church of Christ, expects to provide new adult materials in 1968 with additional materials scheduled for 1969 and 1970. The American Baptist Church plans to introduce a new curriculum in 1969. Protestants and Catholics are beginning to emphasize the church's teaching function in cooperation with "instructed" parents. These significant advances, however, will be ineffective until parish pastors and their official boards come to grips with the fact that *they* must teach "teachers" to teach.

The biblical precedent for teaching is unmistakably clear. The apostles ceased not to preach and *teach* daily. Persuasive gospel preaching motivates and enlightens; relevant evangelical teaching informs and equips. The pastor and the lay leaders must learn to view themselves not only as proclaimers, counselors, and administrators (decision-makers) but also as *teachers*. Conversion and growth in Christian personhood require a complete ministry. The layman has a right to expect the ordained minister to be a faithful student and a competent teacher of the Bible.[12] The minister has a right to expect the laity to seek biblical teaching. He has the obligation to require his leaders to accept teacher education. But pastoral teaching in the parish is not only specific, it is also pervasive. It is not only a task; it is also a temper of mind, an attitude, a stance.

The pastor—with or without a staff—will teach steadily as he preaches.[13] The day of the "pulpit

[12] The reader will recall the emphasis in Chap. 2.
[13] A magnificent example of this dual thrust, preaching-

personality" is over. Thousands of contemporary
clergy meet sizable congregations week after week,
year in and year out, because they are *teaching*
preachers. They experience dry seasons but they never
run dry, because they do not strive to be original,
clever, or showy. Instead, they work to expound the
Bible in the context of contemporary life; they work
to channel God's Word through their human words.
Their parishioners are motivated and enlightened by
the Holy Spirit because they are nurtured from the
Word.

But the renewal pastor is also active in the church's
teaching ministry. *He* teaches confirmation classes,
new members' classes, adult Bible study groups, and
small groups on days other than Sunday. Formally
and informally, he teaches his official board members
and lay teachers in the congregation. The parish pastor who accepts Jesus' teaching ministry as a norm
teaches as he counsels, visits in the parish, and appears
in the community as guest speaker and panelist—
and everywhere as a *Christian* citizen.[14] He encourages and equips the members to teach, too. The
ordained minister is not the only teacher in the congregation, nor necessarily the most competent, but he
is the *chief* teacher. He teaches and equips others to
teach. This function of ministry is positively indispensable to parish renewal.[15]

Preaching from the pulpit—publicly motivating

---

teaching, is Helmut Thielicke, *The Waiting Father* (New York:
Harper & Row, 1959).

[14] See *Preaching and Parish Renewal,* Parts III and IV.

[15] Describing renewal in a downtown church, the writer
devoted three chapters in eight to the place of the *teaching*
ministry. See *From Tradition to Mission,* chaps. 3, 4, and 5.

others to tell the old, old story—is an essential strand in pastoral leadership. But the motivation which the Word stirs in people's hearts can breed confusion unless it is linked with competent evangelical teaching. Zeal without knowledge is not effective; occasionally it is destructive. One reason for conflict and cleavage in many parishes where the gospel *is* addressed to social issues is the lack of biblical and theological teaching among the parish membership. Any congregation in which the leaders and the members are learning to discern the Word in the Bible and disciplining themselves to accept its authority is enabled by God to face social realities constructively and to live responsibly in a revolutionary era.[16] There is no substitute for patient, steady, competent biblical teaching and serious theological conversation in the parish. It causes pain; it also brings healing. Without effective biblical preaching which motivates and competent evangelical teaching which enlightens, the American parish is irrelevant to contemporary life because it is useless to God. It is the Holy Spirit, working through the Word, who motivates and enables. Preaching and teaching are the human means he employs. It is essential, therefore, that stewards of the gospel be found faithful.

Some pastors are ineffective teachers not because their faith is shallow or because their concern for persons is thin, but because their education is sketchy. They got through college and theological school without a substantial grounding in the humanities. Increasingly, theological schools are recognizing this, broadening their curricula, and correlating their

[16] See Chap. 5.

course offerings with those in major university centers. This is crucial. In our eagerness to forge *the* alliance of Geneva, Wittenberg, and Rome, we dare not forget that the chasm between the Reformation and the Renaissance still waits to be bridged. Clergy and lay leaders need personal commitment, catholicity of mind, and cultural insight if they are to speak persuasively to this generation of enlightened but fragmented persons.[17] Christ's church needs Christian humanists.

The teaching ministry in any congregation will be strengthened, therefore, if the official board provides its pastor with the means for continuing his theological-secular education, grants a monthly allowance for his purchase of books, and engages in a continuing dialogue with him on the gospel and the world. From bishop to parish pastor, the teaching function of ministry, allowing for luminous exceptions here and there, is shamefully neglected. The Protestant church has many first-rate executives in its parishes and administrative offices. It can point to a respectable bloc of content preachers. But it sorely lacks effective Christian teachers in its parishes, ecclesiastical offices, and professional schools.

Lay leaders in each parish can take immediate steps to rectify this situation. The Protestant clergy can be effective teachers if the laity challenge and encourage them in it. But a vital teaching ministry cannot exist, let alone flourish, in a wasteland of budgets, building, and bickering. The world demands that the church recover its intellect, develop a taste for ideas, think and converse theologically. Constructive revolt in the

[17] See *From Tradition to Mission*, pp. 70-77, 101-16, 118-21.

grass-roots church is overdue. The laity can turn the tide in a single decade. Presently, they are getting what they ask for, and it is not enough.

## THE CARE OF PERSONS

Yesterday's generation of churchmen remembers the parish pastor—as it remembers the family doctor —on a home-to-home, person-to-person basis. He was an affable generalist, not a hard-nosed specialist. Lost somewhere between yesterday's antiquated model and today's gray flannel executive or social actionist is the wholesome minister who, accepting the New Testament norm, desires authentic personhood for himself and others, has "the courage to be," works to fashion a parish where the Word confronts persons through persons, and labors to build a society in which men are free to become whole persons.

Increasingly, the American parish is valued more as a social service agency, a counseling center, or a command post for social actionists than as a sanctuary for worship. The pendulum may swing too far, but this change in climate does not frighten imaginative leaders. Responsible clergy and laity—glad for the new social concern—will see to it that the congregation does not become *simply* a counseling center, a social service agency, or a training center for "specialists" in social action. Where that is happening—and in some places it is happening—the laity are right to be at odds with their leadership.[18] The church exists to worship God and to preach and teach his

[18] For perspective, the reader will recall Chap. 3, section III, on the worshiping-witnessing church. Chap. 5 will enlarge this perspective.

Word, as well as to witness and render priestly service in the world. A maturing church needs specialists in its multifaceted ministry (cooperative urban ministries, academic communities, recreation areas, industrial settings, the military). Most parishes, however, need competent generalists.

Responsible lay leaders, recognizing that the parish church is not simply a training center for revolutionaries or a hospital for broken persons or a sanctuary for neurotics, will encourage their clergyman to be a competent generalist—preacher, teacher, priest, counselor, friend. They will question whether any parish minister should be called to serve exclusively as *the* director of Christian education, *the* pastoral counselor, *the* administrator, or *the* preacher. This neat division looks appealing on the organization chart, but in practice it fractures the biblical image of ministry. It curtails a man's growth in Christian personhood, because it exalts one function of ministry above another. It tends toward the mechanical. It is arbitrary, artificial. Staff ministries call for assigned areas of responsibility, but each minister must be involved in the church's whole ministry. A senior pastor who preaches but never teaches, counsels, visits, or evangelizes becomes a *personage* rather than a *person* in the parish. But a generalist in the Christian ministry is *not* a jack-of-all-trades. He is herald, teacher, pastoral counselor, general administrator, friend. That is enough to occupy the talents and energies of any man!

This brings another question on leadership into focus. Is there an optimum size for the parish? That must be determined pragmatically according to the

competence and commitment of the parish's clerical
and lay leadership, its geographic location, and its
relevance in the social structure of the community it
serves. But, generally speaking, few parishes with
less than six hundred adult members and a staff of
four to six (clergy and lay) are likely to provide a *comprehensive ministry-in-depth* which nurtures its members for the exercise of Christ's ministry and equips
them to do it in today's pluralistic culture. The several-
hundred-member congregations which constitute the
contemporary Protestant church in America are
luxuries in a mobile society—urban, suburban, or
rural. They exist because of romantic notions, ecclesiastical inertia, and human perversity. The Industrial Revolution called for, and the Urban-Secular
Revolution demands, not only relevant ministry
but effective ministry. A responsible stewardship
of personnel and money is clearly called for. Cooperative ministries, mergers, and "church closings," therefore, testify to a denomination's integrity as well as
its realism. Looking critically at the American parish,
sensitive churchmen are haunted by the Lord's acid
judgment: "The sons of this world are wiser in their
own generation than the sons of light."

We are not suggesting that bigness in itself is good.
The large parish has built-in risks. But current economic, cultural, and personal realities demand it. And
there is cleansing in it. America's thousands of little
parish "clubs"—where prima donna clerics and laymen who revel in "church work" perform for each
other while the world ignores them—are wicked.
Triviality in the name of Christ is sin. Clergy should
live and work together in the same parish and in

cooperative ministries *across* denominational lines.[19]

Equally, laymen who enjoy church work in their little parishes should be thrown into vigorous congregations where several hundred competent people who *don't* like church work do it effectively because it *must* be done if the Word is to go out to all people. This close association might press them to a reappraisal of the gospel, the world, and themselves. The homogeneous parish provides the wrong kind of "sanctuary" for the wrong people. It is a ready-made haven for neurotics, iconoclasts, and extremists. Tension in a congregation should come from the gospel's demands on man and society, not from bickering over the distribution of the Easter flowers or arguing over who should attend convention this year or who should be president of the Ladies' Aid.

In some places the parish clergy are the bottleneck to merger negotiations between parishes and to the fashioning of cooperative ministries across denominational lines. Their subversive activities go unchecked because indecisive and insecure ecclesiastical officials prefer pronouncements to confrontation and practical action. There is grime on the walls of the sacristy. But many lay leaders are equally guilty. Failing to get the recognition in the world which they feel they deserve, some demand it in the innocuous parish church; they want to be big fish in little ponds. Both clergy and lay leaders must be challenged to examine their motives for churchmanship; they must be confronted boldly by realities. Tension will mount! There is much land to be possessed for Christ inside ecclesi-

[19] Stephen Rose, *The Grass Roots Church* (Apex ed., Nashville: Abingdon Press, 1968), addresses this problem head-on.

astical boundaries before the world will listen to the gospel.

Another area for self-examination in every parish calls both the laity and clergy to examine and face those situations where *each* views the *other* as object rather than as subject. How does the American parish regard its clergy—as bold spokesmen for God or as managers paid to serve the corporation? How does the official board view its staff? Do they see them as hired hands to be had at the lowest salaries possible? Shall the senior pastor be a "servant" in economic terms, the associate pastors exploited at minimal wages and then sent on their way, the secretaries paid less than those in the business world, and the sextons and housekeepers chosen simply because they need the money? In those congregations which believe that "the laborer deserves his wages," the official board provides an adequate staff, reviews their competence periodically, and remunerates them accordingly. Where that is not possible—and it is not possible in economically deprived areas and in "mission" congregations—the denomination will subsidize those ministries responsibly or deny them existence.

Secular man disdains a church which provides sanctuary for the incompetent. He also recoils from a church which expects responsible laborers to live in a ghetto of economic hardship. In too many cases, in spite of recent advances, the church practices a "business ethic" which is inferior to that of the responsible business community it often criticizes. The intitiative for change rests primarily with the laity.

But too many clergy also view the laity as objects. Some pastors lament the limitations of the laymen entrusted to their care instead of instructing, challenging, and shepherding them. Some expand church facilities at the expense of the congregation's vital witness. Too many manipulate church members in the interests of a successful institution. Each parish pastor and church executive must face the "professional" schizophrenia which separates preaching from pastoral ministry, teaching from pastoral counseling, the responsible administration of an institution from the pastoral care of persons. Unless the parish pastor sees himself as the man called and ordained to help people meet Christ in the Scriptures, in worship, and in life—and as the man called to develop lay leaders who accept the authority of God rather than of men —the congregation he serves will not exercise Christ's ministry.

The church is not a democracy. It is a free association of persons who, exercising their freedom, accept the authority of God and seek to serve him. It is a voluntary band of servants who demonstrate that Christ is Lord. Only as members meet the living Word in worship and through persons in preaching, teaching, dialogue, and service will some get involved creatively with persons in God's world. Secular man is restless, empty, seeking. The church must present Christ so that secular *and* religious man's deep-seated longing for security and adventure is addressed existentially. The living Word meets man at every point of human need. Christ is man's best and only hope. It is the church's task to present him.

In spite of the harsh things which are said about youth today, the fact is that many want vocations which offer meaning and purpose. Youth can be attracted by and to a living, vigorous, relevant church. That places the responsibility on this generation of clergy and lay leaders to attract, persuade, and equip the present generation of serious youth so that they will witness in a society where so many people insist on freedom without discipline and seek pleasure without purpose.

The issue of leadership must be faced squarely in and by the church. The need for it and its far-reaching personal implications must be admitted candidly and addressed compassionately if parish renewal is to happen. If, finally, any parish pastor or any member of an official board or any ecclesiastical executive is not equal to speaking the truth in love to others *and* hearing it spoken to him, and is not equal to standing firm for Christ and being flexible in all else, he has in fact relinquished his place of leadership. Conviction, compassion, and decision are inseparable in Christian leadership.

Leadership in the church roots first in man's fidelity to the Word of God. It is not by the words of any man—ordained or lay—that the issues of life are met creatively, but by each man's fidelity to the living Word. Biblical knowledge, Christian conviction, and personal decision demonstrate a man's fidelity to the Word. Luther studied the Scriptures. His conscience came under the authority of God. He acted decisively. Leadership in the church requires authentic personhood in Christ.

Second, leadership roots in hard work. Pastoral work is not ecclesiastical busyness. It is not fiddling with forms, playing with organizational patterns, and fussing over agendas. It is not identified with interminable meetings, mimeograph machines, and organized discussions on parish renewal. These church activities have become respectable ways *in the church* to avoid facing reality *in the world*. Pastoral work is anguished wrestling with the Word of God in concrete situations, learning to let that Word confront persons through one's own person, and accepting God's authority over one's own person.

Third, leadership in the parish requires long seasons of earnest prayer. Parish renewal simply does not occur where the clergy and lay leaders neglect petitionary and intercessory prayer. The American parish has not because it asks not. The leadership in most parishes places its *primary* confidence in human plans and attractive programs rather than in persistent prayer in the name of Christ. Creative parish leadership depends heavily on prayer.

Finally, effective leadership in the parish calls for constructive patience. The leaders work for the kingdom; they also wait for it. Conversion and growth in grace cannot be forced.

Pastoral leadership steadies faltering persons, attracts strong persons, and collides with those who accept any authority other than Christ himself. Leadership which roots in the Word awakens, attracts, and persuades persons to worship and to witness. The religionist and the plumber, the church activist and the lawyer, the pedant and the teacher, the organization man and the butcher—discovering authentic personhood in Christ—become light, leaven, salt. But this radical change in persons happens only where individuals are challenged to decide *for* or *against* Christ, persuaded to deny themselves, and supported in their cross-bearing efforts to follow the Lord into the world. Parish renewal is marked by tension and conflict.

## Questions for Discussion

1.  If leadership resides in the community of persons committed to the Word, what degree of leadership centers in your clergy, elected board members, and other lay leaders?
2.  Identify and discuss cultural images of ministry which prevail in your parish. Be specific.
3.  Discuss Luther's statement: "We are all priests, but we are not all clergymen."
4.  Who preaches (proclaims the Word) in your parish—the clergy or the congregation or both? Be concrete.
5.  Shepherding is preeminently, but not exclusively, the ordained minister's task. Discuss this in the context of your parish.
6.  What are the characteristics of the biblical image of ministry? Is it the ruling image in your parish?
7.  Has your congregation shaped the ministry of your clergy? How? To what degree? Has your pastor shaped the ministry of your congregation? How? To what degree?
8.  What constitutes effective parish leadership? Is it different from leadership in other areas of society? In what way?

# 5

# Creative Conflict

*An isolated man, one who has not become
conscious of the ultimate objective link
binding him to all other men before God,
is an unawakened, immature, even a muti-
lated man.*
—DIETRICH VON HILDEBRAND

*Only the hand that erases can write the true
thing.*
—MEISTER ECKHARDT

Only the dead are at peace with one another. Only
the slain soldiers on the battlefield are excused hon-
orably from the decisive engagements waged there.
The end of tension and conflict is death. Unfortunately, many people, like trained dogs, like to play
dead. During the 1930's the admonition was "Don't
stick your neck out." In the 1940's that was shortened
to "Don't volunteer." During the 1950's people sought
ease in corporate structures, suburban living, and
simplistic answers to complex sociopolitical problems.
The early 1960's brought a season of splendid involvement and constructive protest, but now it appears that we are in retreat. Youth admire those who
maintain their "cool," while some liberals are becom-
ing the new isolationists. But freedom from tension
and conflict is an illusion. Man can reduce the sever-
ity of each by curtailing his personal involvements
(marriage and family life, political decisions, military
commitments, teacher-pupil relationships, doctor-pa-

tient relationships, etc.). He cannot, however, escape these realities altogether until he dies.

Tension, controversy, and conflict are elemental strands in the Christian life, because it *is* life and because commitment to Christ involves a cross. Tension develops when man pits his will against God's will. Conflict comes when people, constrained to serve God in concrete situations, collide with people bent on serving their own interests. That is a dominant theme in Scripture from the Garden of Eden to the Garden of Gethsemane, from the fleshpots of Egypt to the Cross outside Jerusalem. The good news that God has demonstrated humanity's possibilities in Christ and has provided in him the means to realize man's potential does not eliminate tension and conflict; it magnifies both. On one occasion Jesus turned, faced his disciples, and rebuked Peter: "Out of my way, Satan!" he said. "You stand right in my path, Peter, when you look at things from man's point of view, and not from God's" (Matt. 16:23 Phillips). Most American churchmen obscure this biblical perspective. The gospel, the church, and the world cannot coexist without tension and conflict. The worldwide mission of the church might have been stillborn if Paul had not managed a face-to-face encounter with Peter over the universal character of the gospel. The doctrine of the Incarnation emerged from a harsh battle between the Docetists and the adherents of the Apostolic Faith. The Cross demonstrates that the cruel conflict between God and the powers of darkness is real. Liberation and renewal come only by way of the Cross—Christ's and one's own. Tension and conflict are inevitable.

Common tensions and conflicts inherent in the renewal process are readily discernible. In this chapter, we propose to examine them as they occur in the parish bent on renewal, between parishes-in-renewal and static congregations, between parishes-in-renewal and the secular society in which they are situated, and between parishes-in-renewal and their denomination's centers of ecclesiastical administration. These multiple tensions and conflicts interact to produce new pain and fresh travail. Inescapably, they are part of the renewal process. The peace of God that outruns human understanding is not the absence of conflict but the assurance that God can overmatch every facet and consequence of sin.

## THE PARISH

*A.* Critical tensions accompany the efforts of parish leaders and members to achieve an objectively sound and existentially meaningful understanding of the Scriptures' witness to the Word of God (Chapter 2). These tensions increase as the parish leaders and members seek to discern, accept, orient to, and project a biblical image of the church and its ministry (Chapters 3 and 4).

*B.* Tension develops when the Christian teacher demonstrates concretely that basic doctrinal truths are not sets of words to which church members subscribe but descriptions of reality which Christian persons experience. Some members who accept the doctrine of the atonement take offense when the Christian teacher speaks concretely about their sin, and his, in terms of the insensitive attitudes and inhumane practices which mar their community. Many who subscribe to the resurrection of Christ are offended when the Christian teacher points out that the living Christ expects church members to take the world seriously and to deal with persons as they are, where they are.

Tension and conflict result when the defenders of out-moded traditions are challenged by those who seek to introduce new life in the parish. The formalists collide with the existentialists; the traditionalists resist the innovators. The former are often too rigid; the latter are frequently too flexible. Conflict results. Simple matters like providing additional worship opportunities, fashioning more flexible liturgical forms in churches with fixed liturgical patterns, and introducing rich worship forms in nonliturgical congregations can excite and antagonize hundreds of members. But human resistance to change is not peculiar to the Protestant tradition. Some Roman Catholics who do not understand a word of Latin are disturbed by the introduction of English in the mass.

C. Tension and conflict result when the call is issued for a trained and committed teaching personnel in the church school, even though this is an essential tactic in the overall strategy of parish renewal. What is called for specifically is the kind but firm retirement of some persons, the recruitment of new persons, and the periodic exposure of *all* teachers to biblical and theological studies. Confusion and hurt accompany these changes as they become operative at all three levels. If, on the other hand, nothing is done, if the personnel remains unchanged, tension and conflict develop in other quarters of the parish. Alert, concerned, and educated parishioners will no longer tol-

erate "pious sentiment" and "Bible stories." Therefore, the sooner this campaign for competent evangelical teaching is launched, the sooner new life will
surge through the parish. The blind cannot lead the
blind, but no one likes to say so in concrete situations
(Chapters 3 and 4).

D. Tension and conflict occur when the parish
leaders and a few members challenge the social and
color barriers in their parish. As long as this addressment remains academic the tensions are not severe. If
the congregation is located in a changing neighbor-
hood, situational tension becomes acute. Positive action brings outright conflict in most situations—at
least for a season. In some places the conflict has been
so severe that the old-line membership has melted
away. But any congregation—urban, suburban, rural
—which acknowledges the Lordship of Christ will
experience tension and conflict when its members
address the issues of class and race existentially. The
racial revolution has scarcely brushed the church. But
the need to minister to persons across class and color
barriers is urgent. The need for healing and understanding between races is acute. Those who prefer
social exclusiveness and institutional security will resist those who want personal and communal involvement. Decisions which affect the institution will not
be made easily, but the Christian congregation has no
option: "Whoever would save his life will lose it."
Jesus made that judgment, and there is no escaping it
without denying him.

E. Tension races through the parish when the
pastoral leadership challenges moralism and legalism
among the members, many of whom are evangelical

in name only. A preaching-teaching-counseling ministry oriented to the gospel and the realities of human existence draws fire immediately. Hard battles rage for a season. Guerrilla warfare goes on for years. The declaration that the "god of inflexible rules" is dead and the proclamation of the God who seeks people *because* of their infidelities, acts of false witness, and searing prejudices infuriates many "respectable, God-fearing" parishioners. They are not a bit happy to discover that individuals whom they dislike, disdain, or envy are acceptable to God! Some churchmen are quite uncomfortable with the Christian God who forgives their penitent enemies. Their inner conflict will not subside until they accept themselves as sinners and seek God's forgiveness, too. The elder brother occupies a dominant position in most parishes. Jesus' plea, "Father, forgive them; for they know not what they do," has a large place in the doctrines of the church but a small place in the hearts of its members. Facing up to this mean reality brings tension and conflict in the members and among the members. The gospel demands that the issue be faced. Doing so is part of renewal.

*F.* In due season those who struggle to accept the authority of God's Word become, in many parishes, a firm majority. The frustrated minority, a bit frenzied by then, harasses them at every opportunity. As this complex situation develops—and it does where renewal is not a flash in the pan—those who are maturing in the Faith demonstrate it by declining to bicker or retaliate. Every parish has its neurotic fringe which must be answered on occasion, but those occasions are rare. Responsible churchmen do not engage in vendettas against neurotics, and they go on caring even when they cannot cure. Purges occur in political societies, not in the household of God! Consequently, tension is inescapable. On the other hand, there are situations where serious laymen, unable to persuade their fellow members to seek renewal, will unite with a renewal congregation so that they *can be* nurtured to serve in the world. This breeds tension, too—especially in over-churched communities.

G. Bitter conflict occurs in the parish when the leaders—having accepted the gospel's demand to manage material goods responsibly—begin to teach Christian stewardship person to person in the parish. There is no effective substitute for these existential encounters from the pulpit, in the official board, and in every corner of the parish. The purpose is conversion and enlightenment. The Bible clearly states that Jesus spoke steadily and concretely in his earthly ministry about material possessions and money. He spoke on the getting and giving of money because both reveal the condition of man's inner life.

The clerical and lay leaders must be willing to speak out and confront others eyeball to eyeball on this issue. They must proclaim that living for others out of commitment to God's redeeming purpose is every Christian's responsible witness. Christians give because Christ first gave himself for them. Whoever gives casually, gives contemptuously. Insofar as churchmen uphold the purposes of Christ's church and respond to the needs of their brethren, they are channels of God's grace. Basically, stewardship is not a method of raising money. It does not depend on programs, gimmicks, or manipulative devices. Stewardship is the voluntary, glad placement of time, talent, and money at the disposal of Christ so that persons may know and serve him.

The miracle of stewardship occurs in those parishes where there is hard wrestling with the demands of the gospel and an honest management of money by the parish leaders themselves. This allows the leaders to speak openly, directly, honestly. Christ said, "Let your light so shine before men, that they may see your good works and give glory to your Father who is in heaven." A scrupulous avoidance of any word that points to the recognition of the giver will in fact eliminate the possibility of witnessing to stewardship as the Christian is called to do in other aspects of his Christian experience.

*H.* Multiple tensions and conflicts stem from the complex nature of church-state relations. This thorny issue is no longer academic for the American church. Some American laymen who applauded the German minority who honored conscience above the Nazi state have now become the harshest critics of their fellow Americans who oppose the war in Vietnam on grounds of conscience or human dignity. Some of the latter are equally harsh in attacking their fellow citizens who, also under constraint of conscience and human judgment, support their sovereign state's acts of force as political realism in a community of sovereign states. Many American churchmen must look back, not in anger but in shame, on their prejudiced stand in the political election of 1960, their mean-spirited carping (both parties) during the 1964 election, and their non-biblical (presently unconstitutional) insistence that the state, housing a pluralistic society, should favor "their" religion above others in the public schools. Jesus said: "Render unto Caesar . . ." That is easier to quote piously than it is to apply in concrete situations. Parish renewalists apply it concretely.

Parish leaders must challenge those church members who like to hear Stainer's "God So Loved the World," yet prove to be uninformed or perverse obstructionists when their church calls them to act out this saving truth in their community. The illusions of these church people must be shattered by plain speech and bold deeds. The only place where the church *can* witness is in the world. Church members—baptized, confirmed, married, and buried by the church—live in the world. They attend a worship service weekly. Some accept Christian instruction in the church school. A minority study the Bible and pray daily. All spend the other one hundred and sixty plus hours outside the sanctuary, classroom, and closet prayer room. Church people work and play, love and hate, give and receive *in* the world. If they witness for Christ, it is in the world or not at all. God moves in human experience; he acts in the course of human history. This is the biblical faith; it is the heart of the gospel. "In Christ God has turned the world over to man." [1] He wants it remade; justice is the sociopolitical expression of Christian love. One's love of God enables him to love his brother. Protestant ministers and Roman Catholic priests (and nuns) who participated in civil rights demonstrations during the early 1960's shocked pietists, jolted secular "status quoers," and angered racists. Actually, they simply acted out

[1] Carl Michalson, *The Rationality of Faith* (New York: Charles Scribner's Sons, 1963), p. 138.

the gospel's claim on *them*. The new man in Christ is constrained to bring his fresh insights and maturing judgments to bear on *his* historical situation in order to create a better society for the sake of the kingdom of God.[2]

Since the days of Paul, Christ's church has sought to exercise his ministry for people in the world. Flight from society has appealed to some people in every generation of Christian history. But Scripture demonstrates that the Christian life exists only in community. "Saint" Simeon Stylites, perched on a pole for thirty years, amuses the modern churchman until he is reminded pointedly that his opposition to his church's discussion of politics and economics, race and class, housing and slum clearance makes Simeon look like a crusader! The Amishman—bearded, hardworking, devout, and withdrawn from the world— has his counterpart—*sans* beard, *sans* hard work, *sans* piety—in every Protestant denomination today.

In Chapter 2 we discovered that this social inertia roots partially in a wrong view of Scripture which informs and nurtures a subjective piety. This in turn is complicated by deep cultural faults in most Protestant lay circles. On both counts, however, many of these laymen deserve to be challenged and enlightened rather than castigated. Too many socially concerned clergy become unnecessarily impatient with parishioners committed to their pastoral care. A few recalcitrant members need to be jarred severely. But many members will respond to patient, pertinent, practical teaching from the resources of the Word.

[2] Daniel D. Williams, *God's Grace and Man's Hope* (New York: Harper & Row, 1950).

Some clergy, preoccupied with devising new forms and involved with needful social reforms, neglect their prior call to preach and teach the Word of God effectively to persons in their pastoral care. Some social actionists in the church deny the biblical faith as neatly as hidebound traditionalists.

But the problem is not only biblical and cultural. It is also theological and personal. The American churchman has a thin awareness of evil.[3] He does not regard sin as chasmic estrangement from God. He does not consider it to be an inner fragmentation of his person, an inborn condition which only God can cure. American Protestants do not see sin as *ignorance* in the perspective of God's Truth, *wickedness* in the light of God's righteousness, *mortality* in the face of God's eternality. Preoccupied with symptoms, they give slight attention to the *cause* of their human predicament. They scarcely recognize that it is further complicated by time of which one never makes the best use, by one's limitation to a particular place at any given moment, and by everyman's enmeshment in the web of human association.[4] Man's inner condition (sin) and his historical predicament (sin) present human problems which no human being (political leader, mate, or counselor) can resolve. Only God can liberate man from sin. But to proclaim this good news concretely is to collide not only with unchurched citizens in the community but also with "decent" church members. It is indeed true, as James Denney once observed, that "the King-

[3] The reader will recall the thrust in Chap. 2.
[4] I am indebted to Werner Elert for this description of Fate (time, place, and the web of human association).

dom of God is not for the well-meaning but for the desperate."

The church exists to confront man in his sin, convince him of it, and offer him liberation through Christ. When this confrontation and offer are accomplished effectively, the preacher and lay leaders come face to face with people whose sin is despoiling life in specific situations. Human ignorance constrains the church to speak publicly on particular political issues whenever its weight threatens to destroy the commonweal (extremism). Wickedness concreted in people who own slum properties in racial ghettos and in those who oppose open housing calls for prophetic confrontation as it did in the eighth century B.C. This addressment of the Word to specific political issues and concrete socioeconomic situations in one's own community infuriates many people and alienates others. Consequently, the parish leaders must remember that biblical preaching and teaching cannot be measured by the plaudits it receives or the dollars it collects but on the basis of how many persons it persuades to decide *for* or *against* Christ. Biblical preaching is worldly preaching. It produces tension and stirs conflict. T. R. Glover once observed that the early Christians were always getting into trouble. Jesus was jarringly plainspoken on this point: "The hour is coming when whoever kills you will think he is offering service to God" (John 16:2).

When persons let Christ appeal through their words and deeds, sharp differences spring up between them and the world. Differences also develop among Christians themselves over how the witness shall be made and which segments of society should be addressed first. Tension develops in the ranks of the faithful, because Christian men and women differ greatly in their maturity of faith, native intelligence, temperament, cultural perception, persuasiveness, and courage. Uniformity in witness is simply impossible. Certainly, it is unbiblical to expect it. Honest differences over the style and place of witness do exist among maturing Christians, but all agree that mature Christians will witness concretely according to *their* faith, temperament, talent, and competence.

Once the breakthrough is accomplished in a particular parish and renewal is underway, attrition sets in. That also creates tension. People grow weary in well-doing unless there is daily restoration of the mind and spirit. The congregation-in-renewal attracts, motivates, and enlightens persons: attendances increase, evangelistic work becomes more demanding, the disposition to wrestle with social issues grows more intense, budgets rise, the need for additional staff becomes pressing—the problems multiply on every front. Weariness, complacency, and pride come forward to cause new tensions.

The attacks from the world become more frequent and more severe because hundreds of church members are witnessing vigorously and concretely. Tension and conflict increase. Waves of envy roll in from other religious establishments in the community and the denomination. The pressures mount and the work increases; order for the sake of freedom becomes crucial. And the risk of losing contact with the source of it all, the Word of God, is always present. The new ministry, born by grace, can live only by grace. It slips away unnoticed if parishioners forget under the pressures of accomplishment that the church's ministry is both a gift and a task. It may be easier to be Christian in the midst of hardship than it is to be Christian in the midst of affluence and observable success. New and unexpected tensions come to the renewed congregation simply because it is in renewal.

Tensions also develop between and among parishes in the same community. Congregations in the same denomination, located in the same community, do not mature at the same tempo; tensions develop. Some congregations do not mature at all; conflict develops. Consequently, effective witness in the community requires that the maturing congregations join forces across denominational lines. Situationally, they are constrained to cooperate. King Albert of Belgium declared that Germany's unprovoked invasion in 1914 "cornered" his little nation into heroism. Presently, parishes-in-renewal, and those bent on renewal, are being cornered into ecumenicity. If, in these situations, some parishioners love their parish or denomination more than they love Christ, their parochialism becomes in fact an act of treason against the kingdom of God. These tensions must be acknowledged, faced, and translated into constructive deeds.

## PARISHES-IN-RENEWAL
### AND STATUS-QUO CONGREGATIONS

Little has been written about the tensions and conflicts between and among congregations in the same community. These tensions are real, hurtful, a poor witness in the world. But they do exist. We observed how tension develops between churchmen who interpret Scripture literally and those who take Christ as the interpreter. Knowledgeable Christians expect this tension. The corrosive problem, however, is not the tension itself, but the unwillingness of both groups to admit and to face it. Parishes which view Scripture subjectively and parishes oriented to an objective view of the Bible rarely get together for theological conversation at the grass roots. It is easier for both camps to analyze this problem in their seminaries, write learnedly about it, and discuss it at their own church meetings than it is to tackle it—community by community. The trouble is compounded by the fact that the confessional churches have strong segments committed to a subjective, unscholarly approach to the Bible. Tension and conflict will persist in and between parishes in the same community, corroding the church's witness, until this elemental issue is dealt with candidly. (See Chap. 2.)

There are, unfortunately, meaner tensions which develop between parishes-in-renewal and status-quo congregations in the same community. Some churchmen in settled parish institutions denigrate the ministries in those parishes where renewal is underway. The damage done, by any conservative estimate, is considerable. Covertly and openly, these uninvolved church people advise prospective members to avoid a particular congregation because "they have trouble over the Negro," "they ask for too much money," "they talk politics," "they don't preach the Bible." Meanwhile, these subversives lament that *their* parish resources are limited, that other parishes are competitive, and that ecclesiastical leaders offer no guidance (which is not always true). Laymen in the throes of renewal are irritated and angered by these indignities. Having faced their own limitations, renewalists tend to be impatient with indecisive, whining neighbors who decline to pay the cost of renewal. This deep-seated conflict reveals the need for spiritual growth in *both* kinds of congregations. The former must confess their envy, sloth, and shallow confidence in God. The latter must surmount the subtle temptations to pride which are inherent in their exciting situation. Concerned parish leaders seize these mean experiences in church life at the grass roots to teach the doctrines of sin and grace more precisely and to proclaim Christ's demands and promises more persuasively. Risking abuse from pietists and illusionists, they also point to the uncomfortable reality that repentance is a daily need in every Christian life and in every corner of the church. The Word of God speaks steadily to man in his historical situation, addressing him at all levels of human need. Repentance and gospel faith, inseparable, open the doors to renewal.

## PARISHES-IN-RENEWAL
## AND THE COMMUNITY

It is precisely because the Word of God meets man at every point of human need that tension and conflict develop between the church and the secular community. When the law and the gospel are proclaimed concretely and acted on by some church members, however falteringly, the battle lines take shape. This is true because natural man recoils from meeting God eyeball to eyeball. He prefers to hide (Adam), lie

(Cain), deceive (Jacob), be sensual (David), be let alone (Jeremiah), avoid conflict (Peter)—or die (Judas).

Any congregation which seeks to read Scripture in the light of Christ, works to proclaim his demands and promises in relevant ways, and disciplines itself to live under God's authority, collides with people and institutions whose first loyalty is to self, family, class, race, or dogma (religious, political, economic). Earnest churchmen who accept God's authority in principle are themselves strained to act on it when it comes to deciding their place in a social club which excludes persons on the basis of race or class; selling their house to a Negro when their neighbors object; bucking their corporation when its multiple benefits dull their conscience; criticizing their party's candidate when his views buttress their aspirations and prejudices. When Christ bids church members to follow him into a racial ghetto, a political arena, or a casual family relationship, every serious Christian among them discovers that he needs a firm personal relationship with God through faith in Christ. Paul testifies to everyman's continuing need for grace: "I can do all things in him who strengthens me."

Servants of the Word confront the world in general and themselves in particular with God's Truth. They also confront persons and groups which employ religious language to foster their ultraconservative political views, meanwhile insisting loudly that mainstream Protestant churches are "preaching politics" when they speak out on race, urban renewal, poverty, and international relations. Unless these "religionists" are confronted from time to time—community by community, and parish by parish, and by responsible ecclesiastical leaders—many church members will be misled and serious secular reformers will keep a caricatured image of the church. A plantation aristocracy and insecure farmers used Scripture to bolster their decadent society in 1860. The Third Reich insisted publicly that it existed by the providence of God. Religious language *can* be used to cloak selfishness and malice.

Servants of the Word confront the world, themselves, and ultraconservatives. They also confront ultraliberals whenever these people confuse the kingdom of God with the city of man. Dissent is indispensable to the life of the free society. Social concern is inherent in authentic Christian witness. But each must stand before the tribunal of biblical evidence. Liberty can become license. Compassion unstructured by truth turns to cheap sentiment. When the social critic recognizes no approach except his own, listens to no voice other than that of his own group, mature churchmen will resist him. The living Word is sharper than a two-edged sword. God acknowledges no authority except his own. The church must live under *that* authority. Conflict results on *all* fronts.

Any congregation striving to honor the Word of God rightly and to respect human freedom—including man's freedom to go to hell—faces conflict with any group fanatically seeking their own interests. Wherever the church seeks to be loyal to the Word of God which judges before it heals, there is tension. The church expects conflict; it does not seek it or relish it. There is a difference between creating conflict and creative conflict. The church prays for unity, desires peace, and works for justice among men. The servant of the Word, the secular reformer, and the humanist walk arm-in-arm in many worldly ventures. Bonhoeffer and von Stauffenberg worked and died together in resisting Hitler. William Temple often allied himself with secularists in politics and economics. But there are seasons when the servant of the Word must walk alone; Luther and Thomas More demonstrated that. The secular city is an exciting arena for Christian witness. So are academic communities, the rice paddies of Vietnam, the African bush, the teeming roads of India, and the farms of France. The world is the object and the subject of Christ's work. But no place or society in this world *is* the kingdom of God. That remains a gift and a task.

Christians live *in* the world; they are not *of* the world. They live in the land of the Philistines, dress like the Philistines, work side by side with the Philistines, marry the sons and daughters of the Philistines, but they do not worship the gods of the Philistines, who are the gods of the passing age. They do not let the world squeeze them into its mold. They seek instead to refashion the world after the mind of Christ in them. Obviously, that is a surefire prescription for conflict. Consequently, many churchmen obscure the prescription and some ignore it altogether.

## PARISHES-IN-RENEWAL
### AND THEIR DENOMINATIONS

Tension exists between individual congregations and the association of congregations which constitute the denominational church. Tension is inherent in Christian institutional life as it is in the institutional life of the family, school, corporation, and nation. It is every Christian's responsibility to see that these inevitable tensions are creative. Parishes-in-renewal, however, experience sharper tensions here which must be admitted honestly and addressed realistically if the present "foment in the church" is to mature into renewal.

First, the major denominations and the sects are discovering (as they did in the Civil War, during the modernist-fundamentalist controversy, and in the harsh struggles over the social gospel) how bitterly church people can and do divide over doctrine and social action. It is likely that these tense situations will multiply and worsen before they decline and improve. The United Presbyterians and the Episcopalians have made news on this front as frequently as most denominations in the 1960's, but all denominations—including the conservative bodies—are experiencing their share of tensions. The Lutheran Church in America, for example, went on public display— "warts and all"—with its courageous documentary film, *A Time for Burning.*[5] This unvarnished report on an Omaha congregation's abject failure to meet Negroes as persons is in fact a radical call to repentance across denominational lines. That particular congregation is not an isolated example in the church.

Second, tensions develop between the national church and congregations-in-renewal over member-

[5] The film, produced by Lutheran Film Associates, is available through most denominational centers. The sequel, *A Time for Building,* is also available.

ship policies. The national church, seeking an equitable base for leveling apportionments (benevolence quotas), defines standards which obscure rather than reflect the biblical shape of the church. This entrenched practice in Protestantism offends the minority of congregations where people are wrestling existentially to orient to a membership policy which requires that one declare Christ as God's Son and personal Savior and accept the disciplines of worship, witness, Bible study, and stewardship. Some renewalists question whether *any* mechanical definition on giving is biblical or persuasive. More basically, they question whether any segment of the church—local, regional, national—should determine specific economic quotas. Budgets, honestly and openly determined, are the only proper guide. No formula is ever equitable; none is ever biblical; none is essentially persuasive.[6]

Third, stewardship and evangelism are particular areas of tension between congregations-in-renewal and the national church headquarters. If budgets are to be overmatched, missions established and nurtured, salaries paid, and schools financed, the church must have money. Unless the church is to stagnate, there must be the steady transfusion of new members into the local congregations. These are proper areas of concern for the church at all levels.

But many national church agencies, staffed largely by men who have *not* presided over parish renewal,

[6] The writer has come to this view. The congregation he serves has risen from grudgingly meeting a $5800 annual benevolence quota to the more mature level of a $120,000 annual response (benevolence) without emphasizing any quota at all. *Preaching and Parish Renewal,* pp. 88-97.

gear evangelism and stewardship to the more uninformed and uncreative congregations. The primary means of fostering evangelism and stewardship, therefore, depends on a mechanical combination of programs and materials. The content of the message is largely ignored. Practically, the thrust becomes one of manipulating persons rather than converting them, of patterning congregations rather than teaching them, of programming methods rather than preaching the gospel.

The renewed congregation confronts this mechanical approach to stewardship and evangelism, calling the church to build evangelism and stewardship from the ground up, laying the foundations on a solid and consistent preaching and teaching thrust. The renewed congregation insists that the church-at-large must demonstrate its confidence in the Word of God by making program and material the servant rather than the master of that Word.

As laymen and clergymen alike speak to this issue in general church meetings, they are often misunderstood. The renewalists' quarrel is not with the offices (functions) of stewardship and evangelism. Their quarrel is more elemental. Having reexamined their parish structures and recast them to provide simple and direct means which get Christ and people together, the renewalists are impatient with and critical of the proliferation which characterizes these Protestant structures and the jargon they turn out. The renewalists do not object to centers of authority under the Word. They object to gray bureaucracies which depend on program and method rather than message and persons.

Fourth, congregations which pursued renewal in the 1950's discovered that many of the then existent church school materials were irrelevant, nontheological, unbiblical. Most denominations have remedied or are remedying that serious fault (Chapter 4). Consequently, new tensions are developing because the national church is ahead of many of its parishes. Some congregations—reluctant to face radical changes in their teaching personnel—are complaining that the material is "too advanced," "not biblical," "revolutionary." The tension will become more acute before it eases, and the danger is that an imaginative leadership may retreat.

Fifth, there are other tensions between the parishes-in-renewal and the centers of ecclesiastical leadership. The only one we want to underscore again focuses on inflexible structures and unimaginative leadership which combine to hinder rather than help parishes which are flirting with renewal. In some cases, isolation and disdain threaten to hurt both the parish and the national church. But in most cases, the congregations-in-renewal, while making sharp criticisms, provide the church-at-large with money, ideas, personnel, and dynamic examples.

## TOMORROW'S TENSIONS

New areas of tension and conflict will emerge on all fronts as congregations-in-renewal address the Word imaginatively to people caught in a mounting cultural revolution of incalculable proportions. The civil rights revolution, metropolitan sprawl, urban renewal, and attritional warfare are current realities which most congregations have not gotten abreast of at all. The present situation, therefore, is critical. Meanwhile, change goes on at an awesome pace. Some congregations-in-renewal and denominational "task forces" are initiating studies to devise means to serve persons in the decades ahead, but these thrusts are tentative, timid, limited. Once again, "the sons of this world (the secularists) are wiser in their own generation than the sons of light."

First, the church must face people's inability to employ leisure time creatively. Within a decade or two, millions of people will be working a three- or four-day week. Many, having three or four full days on their hands, will be devastated; they are at a loss now to employ one day creatively! The problem is staggering in a culture where so many people already pursue pleasure without purpose and employ leisure without zest.

Second, radical changes in the patterns of employment are occurring as automation surges into all areas of production, management, distribution, and communication. What positive word will the church offer in the rising controversy over a guaranteed annual wage? How will it deal with persons who find no significance in their work? How will it address those people whom electronic technology is reshaping? [7]

Third, can the church—which missed a place of leadership in the racial revolution of the 1960's— mature so rapidly that it will be able to lead creatively in the new revolution which is shaping up between

[7] See McLuhan, *Understanding Media: The Extentions of Man,* and the report of the Carnegie Commission on Educational Television, *Public Television: A Program for Action* (New York: Bantam Books, 1967).

the technically skilled and the unskilled throughout the world? Will the church speak relevantly to this emerging new class in America—the "meritocracy" (those who possess the know-how)?

Fourth, will the church fashion effective ways to evangelize persons in those cultures which are thoroughly informed by paganism, Communism, Mohammedanism, Hinduism, and Buddhism?

Fifth, can the church speak healingly to persons in an American society where family stability is shattered by one divorce in every four marriages and harsh human relationships maim persons in one of every two homes? Can it speak to those who separate sex not only from marriage but also from love?

Sixth, the pressures and problems posed by an old-age culture and a youth culture have engulfed an unprepared church. Can it offer more than institutional programs for the former and occasional retreats and moral platitudes for the latter?

Today is intimidating. Tomorrow threatens to be overwhelming. Whatever the church's tactics might be (critical cooperation with secularists), its strategy must be fixed: confidence in the living Word and a disciplined willingness to let Christ confront persons through persons. Every member in any congregation anywhere is free to do that. The results are in the hands of God. He requires only that his stewards be found faithful. But Christian faith—critical, flexible, daring—exists only *in* the world.

## SUMMARY STATEMENT

This little book—written for laymen, parish pastors, seminarians, and bishops who shepherd—

reflects the experience and insights of hundreds of lay and ordained churchmen across denominational lines. It raises many specific questions; it presents firm answers to some and suggests experimental answers to others.

The argument is simple: God's strategy calls for the Word (Christ) to confront persons in their freedom through persons exercising their freedom. This strategy requires that the clergy and lay leaders, like military field commanders, adapt and devise tactics to fit the terrain and situation. The steady secularization of Western society since the Enlightenment, the galloping secularization of American society since 1890, and the revolutionary spirit abroad in every corner of the world have fashioned a new freedom in which a renewed church *can* witness relevantly. But it needs to learn to live with change, ambiguity, and dilemma. It needs to learn that its tactics must vary from culture to culture, community to community, parish to parish —and in the same parish across a single decade. The renewed church ventures, dares to offer answers, experiments, and risks mistakes, because it has confidence in the promises and demands of God, and because it reads the signs of the age accurately.

It is fitting that this study book for laymen should conclude with the plain challenge of a concerned cosmopolitan layman in Christ's church, John S. Badeau.

In the end it is the parish ministry which holds the secret of Christian effectiveness. I am a director of Union Theological Seminary. I was disquieted and shocked to hear at our last directors' meeting that slightly less than half of the students who enter Union Theological Seminary plan to go into the parish ministry. For the seminary community across the United States, I am told that the figure is even lower—only about one-third look forward to finding their profession in the local church. Scholarship, teaching, social action appear to be more attractive to students entering the ministry as instruments of Christian witness and Christian service than the parish ministry and preaching to congregations. And yet it is the congregation which is the body of Christ, and it is in the congregation that must be wrought those changes in human conduct to which the gospel speaks to the world, and no amount of clerical activity in peace marches, civil rights demonstrations, or secular affairs can substitute for them.[8]

But to worship the God of the prophets, the Father of Christ, is not an avenue of escape or a rule of safety. Christian worship motivates and equips the worshiper to speak for God here and now. It constrains and enables the worshiper to accept Christ's Lordship and follow him into the world.

So we end on the note on which we began: the risk of vulnerability. Jesus put the issue of renewal cleanly: "Are you able to drink the cup. . . ?" Each decides that for himself.

## Questions for Discussion

1. Is one ever altogether free from conflict in this life? Discuss this in terms of economic, political, and social experience.

[8] Badeau is Director of the Middle East Institute of Columbia University and a member of the Board of Directors of Union Theological Seminary (New York). He served a tour of duty as U. S. Ambassador to the United Arab Republic. The address from which the quote comes was delivered at Andover Newton Theological Seminary on Friday, September 30, 1966.

2. Identify areas of conflict in your parish. Are these conflicts wholesome or neurotic?

3. Can you identify any controversy or conflict in your parish which stems from persons' *fidelity* to the Word of God?

4. Is it really possible to have a conflict of principles without a conflict of personalities? Why?

5. When one declares that "the American churchman has a thin awareness of evil," do you agree? Discuss your judgment in the context of your parish, community, and person.

6. Why does a status-quo congregation feel threatened by a congregation in renewal? Why is the latter impatient with the former? Be specific.

7. Is Christ at work in the secular city? the rice paddies of China? your community? Be concrete.

8. Is your congregation part of the problem or part of the answer in your community? And you—*quo vadis?* Where are *you* going?

5000